# The Standup Trainer:

Techniques from the Theater and the Comedy Club To Help Your Students Laugh, Stay Awake, and Learn Something Useful

## by Ellen Dowling, Ph.D.

Illustrations by Lynn Maderich

**The Standup Trainer**

Library of Congress Catalog Card Number: 95-083962

ISBN: 1-56447-033-4

Illustrations by Lynn Maderich.

**Ordering information:** Books published by the American Society for Training and Development can be ordered by calling (703) 683-8100. This book can also be ordered from Creative Training Techniques Press (612) 829-1954.

This book is dedicated to my frequently entertaining,
often funny, and always much loved son—
Brando Weldon


And to my parents, John and Pat Dowling,
for passing on the humor genes!

# Special Thanks...

...to Helen F. Moody, my inestimable business partner and dearest friend, who read the first draft of this book and told me to start all over again.

...to the many members of the American Society for Training and Development who participated in the "Standup Trainer" workshops at chapter meetings and regional conferences, especially my dear friends and supporters, Linda Kotkin (Ft. Worth, Texas) and Pat Sweeden (Arkansas), and all those Albuquerque, New Mexico, ASTD members who played "Gorilla Theater" with me in the courtyard of the Four Seasons Hotel.

...and to the anonymous participant who, after attending one of my ASTD workshops, wrote on the evaluation form, "Can't you people find some *normal* trainers?!"

Thanks to you all for teaching me how not to be normal.

# About the Author

Ellen Dowling has been knocking 'em dead in the classroom, training room, auditorium, comedy club, and community theater for over 25 years. She has been a high school teacher, a college professor, a folk-singer, an actor, a playwright, a director, and a standup comic.

Currently, Dr. Dowling is co-owner of The Professional Training Company, a communication skills training and consulting firm. She develops and conducts one-, two-, and three-day programs in writing, public speaking, and interpersonal communication skills for professionals in business, industry, and government.

A long-time member of the American Society for Training and Development (ASTD), Dr. Dowling has served as a former chapter president and assistant regional director for the organization. She has conducted "Standup Trainer" workshops all across the country. She is listed in *Who's Who in the West*, *Who's Who in Education*, and the *World's Who's Who of Women*.

She and her partner, Helen Moody, Ph.D., can be reached at The Professional Training Company, P.O. Box 2578, Corrales, New Mexico 87048; 505/898-9474.

# Introduction

I first met Ellen Dowling at a Region 7 ASTD conference that was being held in Shreveport, Louisiana. That was nearly eight years ago. We did Karaoke at that conference. Ellen's performance shows me that the title and content of this book make perfect sense.

Some of us are trainers by design; others by accident. At times we are fortunate enough to have eager, willing participants in our classrooms — and then there are the days that we wish we had stayed in bed. We don't always (or perhaps never) have that choice. As the saying goes — the show must go on.

This book is built on the premise that you want to do quality training. You want your training to produce results. It recognizes that the adult learner of today is different than the adult learner of a generation ago. Today we are bombarded by a wide variety of media. It seems as though almost everything we see or do is done at an incredibly rapid pace. And we expect that kind of pace in the classroom.

When's the last time you saw on an evaluation, "I wish there was more lecture?" Not very often. Why? Because lecture connotes dull, dry, boring — and we don't need any more of that. That's why the skills of theatrical performers and standup comics can be adapted to spice up our presentations. There is some information best transmitted through the medium of standup presentation. That doesn't mean it has to be dull, dry, or boring. It can just as easily (if you follow Ellen's suggestions) be fun, interesting, and stimulating. The choice is ours.

Each of us needs to realize that our audiences constantly expect us to take what we're doing to the next level. They are expecting continuous improvement, just as we might expect from other parts of the organization.

This book, along with the other resources that Ellen suggests, can help you lay a solid foundation for taking your presentations and training to the next level. If you are new to presenting, the suggestions Ellen offers can help eliminate some of the butterflies every new trainer (and a lot of old ones) experiences.

If you are more experienced (or at least think you are!), Ellen's strategies can help you keep your presentations fresh so that you stay interested and focused as you present your content.

Whether you are a novice or a veteran, however, let me underscore one important fundamental — preparation. Creativity, energy, and impact are most easily generated in your classroom when you have prepared to be creative, innovating, and involving. So don't just read this book with the belief that the concepts are going to find their way into your presentation by osmosis — they won't. But advanced planning can help you create a handout that will involve people. It will help you design activities that will involve your participants so that they are not passive observers, but active learners. You can choose to create an environment that'll help motivate your learners to go beyond the old rote memory to learning with a practical application.

*Bob Pike*

Bob Pike, C.S.P.
President, Creative Training Techniques

# Table of Contents

Special Thanks . . . . . . . . . . . . . . . . . . . . . . . . . . . . . . . . . . . . . . . . . . . . . . . i

About the Author . . . . . . . . . . . . . . . . . . . . . . . . . . . . . . . . . . . . . . . . . . . ii

Introduction . . . . . . . . . . . . . . . . . . . . . . . . . . . . . . . . . . . . . . . . . . . . . . iii

Prologue . . . . . . . . . . . . . . . . . . . . . . . . . . . . . . . . . . . . . . . . . . . . . . . . . 1

    Qualified Reader Self-Test . . . . . . . . . . . . . . . . . . . . . . . . . . . . . . . . . 3

    Who Should Read This Book . . . . . . . . . . . . . . . . . . . . . . . . . . . . . . . 4

    How To Read This Book . . . . . . . . . . . . . . . . . . . . . . . . . . . . . . . . . . 5

    What You Will Learn. . . . . . . . . . . . . . . . . . . . . . . . . . . . . . . . . . . . . 7

    Education vs. Entertainment . . . . . . . . . . . . . . . . . . . . . . . . . . . . . . . 8

    What Standup Comics, Stage Actors, and Trainers Have in Common . . . . . . 10

        Spontaneity . . . . . . . . . . . . . . . . . . . . . . . . . . . . . . . . . . . . . . 10

        Audience Feedback . . . . . . . . . . . . . . . . . . . . . . . . . . . . . . . . . 11

        Reviews. . . . . . . . . . . . . . . . . . . . . . . . . . . . . . . . . . . . . . . . . 11

        Audience Rapport . . . . . . . . . . . . . . . . . . . . . . . . . . . . . . . . . . 12

        A Stage "Persona" . . . . . . . . . . . . . . . . . . . . . . . . . . . . . . . . . . 13

        Memorizing Lines . . . . . . . . . . . . . . . . . . . . . . . . . . . . . . . . . . 13

        Length of Performance . . . . . . . . . . . . . . . . . . . . . . . . . . . . . . 14

        The Stage Environment . . . . . . . . . . . . . . . . . . . . . . . . . . . . . 14

    The Standup Trainer . . . . . . . . . . . . . . . . . . . . . . . . . . . . . . . . . . . 16

Act One: Getting Your Act Together . . . . . . . . . . . . . . . . . . . . . . . . . . . . 17

    Objective . . . . . . . . . . . . . . . . . . . . . . . . . . . . . . . . . . . . . . . . . . . 19

    Preparing for Your Standup Training . . . . . . . . . . . . . . . . . . . . . . . . . 20

    1. Creating and Developing Your Training Persona . . . . . . . . . . . . . . . . . 21

        Dress for Your Persona . . . . . . . . . . . . . . . . . . . . . . . . . . . . . . 27

    2. Creating and Developing Your Material . . . . . . . . . . . . . . . . . . . . . . 31

        Tell Stories . . . . . . . . . . . . . . . . . . . . . . . . . . . . . . . . . . . . . 31

        Stories for Trainers . . . . . . . . . . . . . . . . . . . . . . . . . . . . . . . . 33

        Train With Examples. . . . . . . . . . . . . . . . . . . . . . . . . . . . . . . . 37

        Analyze Jokes Carefully . . . . . . . . . . . . . . . . . . . . . . . . . . . . . 40

        Collect Quotes . . . . . . . . . . . . . . . . . . . . . . . . . . . . . . . . . . . 43

        Some Quotable Quotes for Trainers. . . . . . . . . . . . . . . . . . . . . . 43

    3. Tailoring Your Persona and Material to the Audience . . . . . . . . . . . . . 47

        Tailor Your Persona . . . . . . . . . . . . . . . . . . . . . . . . . . . . . . . . 47

        Tailor Your Material . . . . . . . . . . . . . . . . . . . . . . . . . . . . . . . 47

4. Rehearsing Your Performance . . . . . . . . . . . . . . . . . . . . . . . . . . 50
    Rehearse Before a "Real" Audience . . . . . . . . . . . . . . . . . . . . . 50
    Check Your Timing . . . . . . . . . . . . . . . . . . . . . . . . . . . . . . . . 50
    Anticipate Your Audience . . . . . . . . . . . . . . . . . . . . . . . . . . . 51
5. Revising and Adjusting Your Material and Your Persona . . . . . . . . . . . . 53

Act Two: Polishing Your Technique . . . . . . . . . . . . . . . . . . . . . . . . . . 57
  Objective . . . . . . . . . . . . . . . . . . . . . . . . . . . . . . . . . . . . . . . . 59
  1. Improving Your Vocal Delivery . . . . . . . . . . . . . . . . . . . . . . . 61
    Speak Up! . . . . . . . . . . . . . . . . . . . . . . . . . . . . . . . . . . . . . . 61
    Add Vocal Variety . . . . . . . . . . . . . . . . . . . . . . . . . . . . . . . . 66
    Control Your Speed . . . . . . . . . . . . . . . . . . . . . . . . . . . . . . . 69
    Overcome Other Vocal Problems . . . . . . . . . . . . . . . . . . . . . . 69
  2. Learning To Move . . . . . . . . . . . . . . . . . . . . . . . . . . . . . . . . 71
    Warm Up and Calm Down . . . . . . . . . . . . . . . . . . . . . . . . . . 71
  3. Adding Appropriate Gestures and Expressions . . . . . . . . . . . . . 76
  4. Keeping Your Focus . . . . . . . . . . . . . . . . . . . . . . . . . . . . . . 81
  5. Making It All Work: Improvising . . . . . . . . . . . . . . . . . . . . . . 89
    Situations for Improvising With Groups . . . . . . . . . . . . . . . . . 91

Act Three: It's Show Time! . . . . . . . . . . . . . . . . . . . . . . . . . . . . . . . 95
  Objective . . . . . . . . . . . . . . . . . . . . . . . . . . . . . . . . . . . . . . . . 97
  1. Interacting With Your Audience . . . . . . . . . . . . . . . . . . . . . . 98
  2. Establishing Immediate Rapport . . . . . . . . . . . . . . . . . . . . . 101
    Ask Questions . . . . . . . . . . . . . . . . . . . . . . . . . . . . . . . . . . 101
    Maintain Eye Contact . . . . . . . . . . . . . . . . . . . . . . . . . . . . . 104
  3. Using the Callback Technique . . . . . . . . . . . . . . . . . . . . . . . 105
  4. Dealing With Difficult Trainees . . . . . . . . . . . . . . . . . . . . . . 108
    Use Your Standup Skills . . . . . . . . . . . . . . . . . . . . . . . . . . . 109

Epilogue . . . . . . . . . . . . . . . . . . . . . . . . . . . . . . . . . . . . . . . . . . 113
  Epilogue . . . . . . . . . . . . . . . . . . . . . . . . . . . . . . . . . . . . . . . . 115
  Dealing with Criticism . . . . . . . . . . . . . . . . . . . . . . . . . . . . . . 116
  Resources for Further Standup Training . . . . . . . . . . . . . . . . . . . 117
  Curtain . . . . . . . . . . . . . . . . . . . . . . . . . . . . . . . . . . . . . . . . 119
  Additional Reading . . . . . . . . . . . . . . . . . . . . . . . . . . . . . . . . 120
  About the Publishers . . . . . . . . . . . . . . . . . . . . . . . . . . . . . . . 122

# Individual/Group Exercises and Checklists

Developing Your Persona . . . . . . . . . . . . . (Individual Exercise) . . . . . . . . . . . . 23

Developing Your Persona . . . . . . . . . . . . (Group Exercise) . . . . . . . . . . . . . . 24

Analyzing Your Role Model . . . . . . . . . . (Individual Exercise) . . . . . . . . . . . . 25

Creating Your Personal Press Release . . . . (Individual Exercise) . . . . . . . . . . . . 26

Analyzing Your Costume . . . . . . . . . . . . . (Individual Exercise) . . . . . . . . . . . . 29

Storytelling . . . . . . . . . . . . . . . . . . . . . . (Individual Exercise) . . . . . . . . . . . . 36

Developing Examples . . . . . . . . . . . . . . . (Individual Exercise) . . . . . . . . . . . . 39

Analyzing Jokes . . . . . . . . . . . . . . . . . . . (Individual Exercise) . . . . . . . . . . . . 42

Collecting Humorous Quotes . . . . . . . . . (Individual Exercise) . . . . . . . . . . . . 46

Tailoring Your Material . . . . . . . . . . . . . (Individual Exercise) . . . . . . . . . . . . 49

Checklist for a Mind Rehearsal . . . . . . . . (Individual Exercise) . . . . . . . . . . . . 52

A Checklist for Continuous Improvement . (Individual Exercise) . . . . . . . . . . . . 54

Projecting Your Voice . . . . . . . . . . . . . . . (Individual Exercise) . . . . . . . . . . . . 63

Projecting Your Voice . . . . . . . . . . . . . . . (Group Exercise) . . . . . . . . . . . . . . 64

Projecting Your Voice . . . . . . . . . . . . . . . (Group Exercise) . . . . . . . . . . . . . . 65

Adding Vocal Variety . . . . . . . . . . . . . . . (Individual Exercise) . . . . . . . . . . . . 67

Adding Vocal Variety . . . . . . . . . . . . . . . (Group Exercise) . . . . . . . . . . . . . . 68

Relaxation . . . . . . . . . . . . . . . . . . . . . . (Individual Exercise) . . . . . . . . . . . . 73

Relaxation . . . . . . . . . . . . . . . . . . . . . . (Group Exercise) . . . . . . . . . . . . . . 74

Gestures . . . . . . . . . . . . . . . . . . . . . . . . (Individual Exercise) . . . . . . . . . . . . 78

Gestures and Facial Expressions . . . . . . . . (Group Exercise) . . . . . . . . . . . . . . 79

Gestures and Facial Expressions . . . . . . . . (Group Exercise) . . . . . . . . . . . . . . 80

Stanislavsky's Concentration Exercises . . . (Group Exercise) . . . . . . . . . . . . . . 84

Concentration Exercises . . . . . . . . . . . . . (Group Exercise) . . . . . . . . . . . . . . 85

Concentration Exercises . . . . . . . . . . . . . (Group Exercise) . . . . . . . . . . . . . . 86

Concentration Exercises . . . . . . . . . . . . . (Group Exercise) . . . . . . . . . . . . . . 87

Concentration Exercises . . . . . . . . . . . . . (Group Exercise) . . . . . . . . . . . . . . 88

Improvisation . . . . . . . . . . . . . . . . . . . . (Individual Exercise) . . . . . . . . . . . . 90

Improvisation . . . . . . . . . . . . . . . . . . . . (GroupExercise) . . . . . . . . . . . . . . 92

Improvisation . . . . . . . . . . . . . . . . . . . . (GroupExercise) . . . . . . . . . . . . . . 93

Improvisation . . . . . . . . . . . . . . . . . . . . (GroupExercise) . . . . . . . . . . . . . . 94

Asking Questions To Establish
Immediate Rapport . . . . . . . . . . . . . . . . (Individual/Group Exercise) . . . . . . 103

Callbacks . . . . . . . . . . . . . . . . . . . . . . . (Individual/Group Exercise) . . . . . . 107

Dealing With Difficult Trainees . . . . . . . . (Individual/Group Exercise) . . . . . . 111

Performance Evaluation Checklist . . . . . . (Individual/Group Exercise) . . . . . . . 118

# Prologue

# Qualified Reader Self-Test

Are you truly qualified to read this book? Find out by taking this simple test. Place a check mark in either the "yes" or "no" box beside each question.

| Question | Yes | No |
|---|---|---|
| 1. Are you an experienced trainer? . . . . . . . . . . . . . . . . . . | ❏ | ❏ |
| 2. Do you believe that substance is—basically—more important than style?. . . . . . . . . . . . . . . . . . . . . | ❏ | ❏ |
| 3. Do you believe that education is more important than mere entertainment? . . . . . . . . . . . . . . . . . . . . | ❏ | ❏ |
| 4. Do you know how to design, develop, and deliver training programs based on sound principles of adult education? . . . . . . . . . . . . . . . . . . . . . . . . . | ❏ | ❏ |
| 5. Do you know how to set clear, *measurable* learning objectives for your trainees? . . . . . . . . . . . . . . . . . . . | ❏ | ❏ |
| 6. Do you know how to ensure that your training programs have direct application back on the job? . . . . . . | ❏ | ❏ |
| 7. Do you believe that no training program—no matter how technical—need be boring? . . . . . . . . . . . | ❏ | ❏ |
| 8. Do you believe that adults learn better when they're awake and interested?. . . . . . . . . . . . . . . . . . . | ❏ | ❏ |
| 9. Are you currently conducting training programs as an internal trainer or external consultant? . . . . . . . . . | ❏ | ❏ |
| 10. Would you like to learn how to add a little "pizazz" to those training programs? . . . . . . . . . . . . . . . | ❏ | ❏ |

# Who Should Read This Book

If you answered "yes" to all 10 questions, you are qualified to read this book. If you answered "no" to any one of the questions, then you're not ready to read this book. (Don't even think of cheating. We have ways of finding you out.) All right, all right. If you didn't answer "yes" to all the questions but you really want to read this book, go ahead. But don't say I didn't warn you!

This book is designed for trainers who already know—through education and experience—that a dramatic delivery style and a theatrical training atmosphere can never substitute for the real purpose of training, which is to teach adults the skills they need to perform their jobs.

If you do not yet know how to design and conduct training programs that teach participants useful, measurable skills, then this book is not the place to start. Go back to the basics. Read Robert Mager's many books on the principles of instructional design. Also study all the volumes in the American Society for Training and Development's *Trainer's Toolkit* series. Immerse yourself in *The Training and Development Sourcebook* or *The Training Trilogy: Assessing Needs, Designing Programs, Facilitation Skills,* both from HRD Press. Enroll in an intensive, hands-on basic skills for trainers workshop. Earn a degree in training and development or adult education. Join ASTD or the International Society for Performance Improvement (ISPI), and attend as many professional conferences as you can. Design, conduct, and evaluate a whole bunch of one-, two-, and three-day training programs. Then add a little extra to your delivery style—a little humor, a little drama, a little performance art.

That's when you'll be ready to read this book.

# How To Read This Book

This book is designed to be both an overview of the "art" of standup training and a practical handbook of exercises to teach you the skills you need to become a standup trainer.

The central metaphor of this book is the theatrical performance. Like stage actors and standup comics, trainers perform on stage before a live audience. Therefore, this book is designed for you to read as you might read a play:

The **Prologue** describes the intended readership, summarizes the objectives of this book, and explores the connections between education and entertainment. It also analyzes the performance elements that standup comics, stage actors, and trainers have in common.

**Act One** sets the stage for a standup training session. Learn how to identify and develop your own stage "persona," as well as how to find or create humorous material for your "act" and "tailor" your persona and material to a particular audience.

**Act Two** thickens the plot. Here you will learn how to vocalize, move, concentrate, and improvise effectively.

**Act Three** pulls it all together. Once you're actually on stage, there's no turning back. You need to know how to "inter-act" with your audience, establish rapport, and deal with "difficult" audience members.

The **Epilogue** (literally, the "last words" of a play) covers how to deal with reviews—both glowing and devastating. It also includes names of places to go and people to see for further standup training and contains a final checklist for assessing your own performance.

Each "act" also includes exercises to practice what you're learning. Some can be completed alone. Others require working with a group. The versatility of this format allows you to use this book as a stand-alone training text or as a supplement to an advanced train-the-trainer program.

Whether using this book for self-development or to train others, please be aware that the exercises are not meant to be ends in themselves. They are the means by which to accomplish the desired end: educating in an entertaining way.

Allow me to stress again that the best trainers use the actor's art to *enhance* the content of their training sessions, not to substitute style for substance. In his book, *The Empty Space,* British theater director Peter Brook says, "I know of one acid test in the theater. When a performance is over, what remains?"

This same "acid" test can be applied to the training session: Your goal is to be interesting enough so that your audience will learn and retain what you've said. Whether conducting training sessions on such topics as ISO 9000 Certification Procedures, Next Year's New Rules and Regulations for Filling Out the Same Old Stupid Forms, or (my personal favorite) Writing Basics: Grammar and Usage, your goal is to keep people awake and alert enough so that they can apply what they learn to their jobs and make a positive contribution to their organization's mission and goals.

"In life you can be boring," Stella Adler says in *The Technique of Acting.* "On stage you cannot afford to be boring, not even for an instant." This book will teach you how not to be boring in the training room.

# What You Will Learn

Students of modern theater are taught to analyze the character they're about to play in terms of that character's objectives. "What does my character want?" a student actor will ponder. "What does Hamlet want? To discover who killed his father...; to get rid of his despised step-father...; to find a makeup cure for his 'inky disposition'...."

Acting students learn that they can't "act" a state of being (Hamlet wants to be melancholy), but they can act an action. (Hamlet wants to make everyone think he's crazy.)

Experienced trainers know they also are supposed to measure a training session's outcome by emphasizing the verbs in their instructional objectives. Before beginning a session, the trainer asks, "What do I want my participants to *do* after the training session?"

Here's what I want you to be able to do after you're finished reading this book:

- Identify and develop your standup "persona."
- Create and develop humorous material.
- Tailor your "act" (your persona and material) to reach a specific audience.
- Improve your vocal delivery skills.
- Move and gesture more dramatically (and humorously).
- Anticipate your audience's reactions.
- Interact with your audience.
- Establish immediate rapport with your audience.
- Use the "callback" technique.
- Deal with "difficult" audience members.
- Review and evaluate your own performance.

It took Hamlet nearly five acts to achieve his objectives. You can achieve yours in three, but only if you're ready to act.

# Education vs. Entertainment

One of my son's teachers complained to me during a parent-teacher conference that students nowadays expect too much from their teachers. "They don't want to learn," he said. "They just want to be entertained. It's not my job to entertain them."

I think he's wrong. I think it is the teacher's job to entertain, as well as educate. In fact, I think the best teachers are also skilled performers. I'll bet you feel the same way, or you might not be reading this book.

Think back to the best teachers you had in school. Didn't they make the material "come alive" for you in some way? Didn't they somehow keep you awake and interested, no matter what the subject? I remember a chemistry teacher who demonstrated the effects of liquid nitrogen by dipping a daffodil in a container of the incredibly cold liquid. He pulled the daffodil out, held it so we could see that it looked exactly the same as before, then flicked his finger at it and shattered pieces of the frozen flower all over the front row. "Imagine what that would do to your finger," he intoned dramatically.

I also remember a French teacher who comically dramatized the inane dialogues we had to memorize by flinging his body against the blackboard as he shrieked in horror, "BONJOUR, JEAN! OUI EST LA BIBLIOTEQUE!" I also was taught by a tiny Filipino nun who kept us awake in Algebra II by telling us ghost stories. And a theater history professor who acted out all the great parts and made the material so interesting that I fell in love with the art of teaching and vowed someday to be a teacher like him.

Actually I first discovered the connection between education and entertainment inadvertently. As a junior at an all-girls' high school, I made my stage debut in *Macbeth* as (who else?) Macbeth. I took my role very seriously. I learned my lines and lowered my voice. I glued a newly-shorn classmate's cast-off hair to my chin, and I practiced striding purposefully and manfully. I went out on stage, scowled fiercely at the audience and intoned, "So foul and fair a day I have not seen," in my profoundest basso. The audience howled with laughter. I was crushed. But I learned to love Shakespeare.

Later, as an assistant professor of English and Theater Arts at Texas A&M University, I discovered ways to keep Aggies awake and interested through two semesters of Freshman Composition and one semester of Introduction to Literature. I learned that a little bit of relevant humor does indeed make the lesson go down easier. And yes, students do learn to appreciate Shakespeare much better if they act out a scene or two, even if they look ridiculous in tights and speak with broad Texas twangs.

When I left academia for the corporate training world, I discovered it was even more of a challenge to keep students alert and interested, simply because the classes were more intensive. Actors on stage need only keep our attention for two to three hours. But we trainers often have to keep participants awake and alert for eight hours a day. We have to keep our trainees' energy flowing at three o'clock in the afternoon, despite the fact that these folks have been sitting in the same uncomfortable chairs, staring at the same windowless walls, alternately shivering or sweating in the same stuffy room since eight o'clock that morning. Typically, we also have to deal with an audience that may not even want to be there; they may have been *sent*.

In my more than 10 years' experience as a trainer, I have learned that a little humor and drama can electrify even the most recalcitrant trainees. I am always pleased when a participant writes on the course evaluation, "Instructor made a boring topic interesting." I believe that means they probably learned something.

When participants are enjoying themselves, they are more receptive to new ideas. When they are having fun, they remember key points. When they are being entertained, they stay awake. Plus, they give you really great evaluations: "Best instructor I've ever had!" "This company should use this instructor more often!" "This class changed my life!"

It works both ways: Teachers and trainers can be entertainers, and entertainers also can instruct. I've always had a particular fondness for standup comics who could make me laugh and teach me something at the same time. George Carlin, for example, cracks me up when he points out the ironies of the English language. ("What does the term, 'odds and ends' mean?" Carlin asks. "If you have 24 odds and ends on a table and 23 fall off, what do you have left? An odd or an end?")

I suspect that Plato may have been one of the first "standup philosophers," combining theory with an amusing and entertaining delivery. And if Fifth Century B.C. audiences wanted more education, they could always go to the theater, where a production of Sophocles' *Oedipus Rex* would teach them about history, mythology, and morality.

Entertainment is not a substitute for education. It is an enhancement. This is the central premise explored in this book.

# What Standup Comics, Stage Actors, and Trainers Have in Common

First, they are all performers. More precisely, they all perform before live audiences.

Thus, it's not surprising that trainees frequently evaluate trainers not on their ability to design an effective training seminar, but on how well they "perform" while delivering a training session. In fact, many trainers have performed in amateur theatricals, and they frequently flock to "train-the-trainer" conferences to learn new techniques for enhancing their "standup" skills.

Let's look at some other aspects of stage work that trainers have in common with actors and comics.

## Spontaneity

Like actors and standup comics, trainers rely on a live audience to keep their presentations fresh. All live performers usually repeat their performances—sometimes many times. Actors may appear in a long-running play, performing the same role in the same play eight times a week for a year or more. Standups, even those who use topical humor, may repeat a tried and true routine over and over. Trainers may teach a course in cultural diversity every other week for several years. Without the constant challenge of a new audience every time, performances can grow stale very quickly.

Konstantin Stanislavsky, father of the technique known as "Method Acting," called this need for freshness in the midst of repetition "the illusion of the first time" *(My Life in Art)*. All other artists, he said, can create their art whenever they personally feel like painting, or sculpting, or writing a novel or a poem. "But the artist of the stage [or of the training room] must be the master of his/her own inspiration and must know how to call it forth at the hour announced on the posters of the theater [or in the training catalogue]."

Did you sleep badly last night? It doesn't matter. You've got to get through that three-day time management seminar in Portland, Oregon, before you catch a plane to conduct a two-day workshop in Albuquerque, New Mexico. The show must always go on.

Mortimer J. Adler also has addressed the "illusion of the first time" in his book, *How To Speak, How To Listen*. "A good lecturer, in short, must have some of the gifts of a good actor. Each time the curtain goes up, no matter how many times it has gone up before for the lecturer, it should always seem like a new performance for the audience."

## Audience Feedback

Comedic actors, standup comedians, and trainers all receive immediate feedback from their audiences.

Standups, of course, depend on hearing laughter or some other response immediately. (In the Comedy Gym Workshop[1] I attended, I was told that comics need to get their first laugh in the first 15 seconds on stage.)

Comic actors also need to hear laughter, or their performance will suffer. "The audience was dead tonight," the actor will complain backstage. "I nearly died out there." (I've always thought that this was a somewhat ironic state of affairs. After all, the actor is supposed to go out on stage and "kill" the audience.) Likewise, if the audience laughs where they're not supposed to (laughing *at* the actor, instead of with the actor), it throws the actor's timing off. In essence, a "good" audience (one that laughs heartily in the right places) can mean the difference between a so-so and a stellar performance that night.

Trainers need feedback even more than standups or actors do, since they can easily see the participants in the training room, and since they sometimes perform for such long stretches of time. Although laughter is not a trainer's primary objective, it is such a positive form of feedback that it immediately improves the trainer's performance. Laughter adds energy to a training session, defuses aggression, calms any qualms, and joins the audience and trainer in a conspiratorial camaraderie. Plus, when they're laughing, you know they're awake!

## Reviews

Actors frequently find themselves at the mercy of theater reviewers who write for publication. Some widely syndicated reviewers wield such power that their evaluations can actually close a Broadway show or seriously impair an actor's career.

---

[1] For more information about the next Comedy Gym Workshop being conducted in your area, contact Sam Cox in Austin, Texas, at 1-800-700-JOKE.

"To a man with a sour stomach," Mark Twain once said, "all the world's a green apple." If you're an actor, it might be just your luck that in a theater full of people laughing their heads off, one spectator—the critic—is feeling rather nauseous.

Standups, on the other hand, are lucky because they get reviewed by everyone, and the majority rules. Standups don't have to make *everyone* laugh to be successful; they just need to make *most* of the audience happy. Standups succeed by word-of-mouth; if at least a large portion of the audience thinks they're hilarious, they'll probably be invited back for future performances.

A trainer also gets reviewed by *all* the training session participants. If one or two participants don't like the trainer's style, they can be overridden by the other 18 who thought it was wonderful. Generally speaking, trainers are content to get a 4.5 or better on their end-of-course evaluations. A perfect 5.0 is fantastic, but not necessary for continued success. Conversely, if trainers get a low score from the majority of their trainees, then they know immediately that they need to do some major overhauling of their act if they expect to stay in business.

A theater reviewer once judged the stage performance of a friend of mine to be "solid, but narrow." The actor wondered what he was supposed to do to improve—get "wider" somehow? One person's opinion may not be useful information for the performer. But when the entire audience gives a similar review, trainers know where they stand. If most of your trainees think you were boring, you know where you need to improve.

## Audience Rapport

Trainers and standups must establish immediate rapport with the audience. Both do this by means of eye contact and conversation.

Standup comics frequently begin their routines by asking the audience such questions as, "How are you all doing tonight? Are you having fun?" If the response is quick and positive, the comic can move easily into the first "bit," confident that the audience is ready to react and laugh.

Trainers frequently use the same technique to begin their training sessions. They ask the participants to share their names and job positions with the rest of the class. They also may ask them to describe what they hope to learn from the session, or what their greatest concerns about the training topic might be. This opening gambit sets up an informal, conversational tone for the session and lets the participants know right away that the trainer is determined to make the session fit their particular needs.

# A Stage "Persona"

Actors do not need to create their parts. They need only interpret the character the playwright has given them. One actor's Juliet may be more passionate than another's, but both are constrained by the dialogue Shakespeare has already written for them.

Standups must create their own stage persona. Indeed, discovering your persona is fundamental to any progress you may make towards becoming a standup. Are you going to be the "wise guy" á la Jerry Seinfeld or a sexy madcap like Sandra Bernhard? Since your persona will dictate your costume, an effective comic persona may result in laughter the minute you walk on stage, based simply on what you look like.

Trainers also need to create a stage persona, but the range of choices is more limited. Essentially, as a trainer you want to aspire to an "expert professional" look and a "knowledgeable yet accessible" style of delivery. To be an effective standup trainer, you need to look somewhat formal and act somewhat informal. (More on this in Act One.)

# Memorizing Lines

What is the number one cause of stage fright among actors? The fear that they might forget their lines. When an actor "goes up" on his or her lines during a live performance, it's a terrible sight to behold. First there's this unnatural pause (to the audience, a few nanoseconds; to the actor, an eternity). Then there's this slightly bug-eyed expression on the actor's face as he or she tries desperately to ad-lib a suitable replacement for the forgotten line. Then there's that same slightly bug-eyed look on the faces of the other actors on stage. Then somebody comes up with something vaguely appropriate, the actors rally, the audience breathes again, and the show goes on. (Junius Brutus Booth, considered by many to be the greatest American actor of the 19th century, once stopped in the middle of a performance, looked straight at the audience, and said cheerfully, "I'm sorry. I seem to have forgotten my part." Arggggh.)

It's similarly scary for standups. They have to memorize their bits, punch lines and all. An ad-lib just may not be funny enough (unless you're Robin Williams). The only advantage standups have over actors when they forget their lines is that they're usually alone on stage. If they forget a bit, or transpose it to another part of their routine, no one will know but them. An actor in a

Shakespearean play can hardly get away with that without the audience knowing that something is wrong. ("Not to be or to be... oops!")

Trainers are lucky. They can use notes! They don't have to memorize anything, and they can transpose and rearrange material to their heart's content. Indeed, sometimes they need to do some mid-session rearranging, in response to their trainees' needs. Stage fright for a trainer? Pshaw.

## Length of Performance

A standup typically performs from six minutes to an hour or so in concert. One minute is a long time on stage if you're not getting any laughs.

Stage actors usually perform in plays that last from 15 minutes (a one-act play) to over 3 hours (a full-length play). Depending on the size of the part, an actor may be on stage for most of the performance, or just a few scenes. One minute on stage is a long time if you can't remember your lines.

Trainers win the performance-stamina award hands down. Trainers sometimes conduct full-day seminars (8 a.m. to 5 p.m.) for three or more consecutive days. At some point, you may have to deal with an audience that just may be plain tired of looking at you!

On the other hand, you don't have to memorize your lines, and you don't *have* to get laughs. You have the luxury of time: time to establish a credible persona, time to get to know the audience, and time to energize and build to a series of training climaxes. If it doesn't kill you first, time is certainly on your side.

## The Stage Environment

Flexibility is the name of the game here. This is true even for actors, who usually perform on a set that they've rehearsed on for at least a few days. However, even familiar spaces can contain surprises for the actor. Stage doors stick or open slowly when they're supposed to stay closed; stage walls, called "flats," sometimes fall on the unwary actor. Or telephones on stage may not ring when they're supposed to or may ring when they're not supposed to. The actor may have to incorporate these unplanned changes in the set into the performance itself. ("I'll just close this door, Madelaine. It's a bit drafty in here.")

Standups work under even less predictable circumstances. Every comedy club is designed differently, so the standup may have to make instant adjustments. For example, one of Murphy's Rules of Comedy is that the microphone will always be a foot too low or a foot too high for you, so you will have to adjust it as you begin your opening bit.

Likewise, trainers never know what kind of a space they may end up in. I've trained in lush training rooms with outside windows, state-of-the-art equipment, ergonomically designed chairs, and acoustically sealed walls. I've also trained in rooms large enough for only 8 people (with 20 in my class) and in rooms that could easily hold 400 people (with only 20 in my class). I've trained in rooms with leaking roofs (drip, drip, drip for eight hours—such a pleasant sound) and rooms with paper-thin walls, which were no match for the jackhammer teams on the other side. I've had to deal with burned-out overheads, permanent markers on erasable whiteboards, used-up flip charts, obnoxious intercoms, and inoperative thermostats. No one needs more flexibility than a trainer!

# The Standup Trainer

Actors can achieve fame and fortune, but they have to memorize their lines and risk public humiliation because of cranky reviewers. Standups also can become rich and famous, but they have to memorize their routines and get a laugh every 20 seconds.

As a trainer, you may not retire as a millionaire or be nationally recognized, but you can teach people new skills and new ideas. Like teachers, trainers "affect eternity."  And you don't have to memorize your lines or get laughs.

I've been an actor, so I know the pleasure of getting applause at the end of a well-received play. I've also been a standup comic; I know the pleasure of getting a laugh at the end of a well-received joke. But as a trainer, I know that nothing beats the pleasure of getting a telephone call several weeks after the training session from a trainee who says, "I used what you taught us in the class and it worked!"

My goal is to show you how to use standup-performer skills to deliver training that *works*.

# Act One: Getting Your Act Together

# Objective

The objective of this section is to present a protocol (a predictable series of steps) for preparing for a standup performance.

Stage actors typically spend weeks rehearsing material that has already been developed by playwrights such as Anton Chekhov or Wendy Wasserstein. During this time, they also develop (with the director's guidance) interpretations of roles that already have been created (e.g., Hamlet, Willy Lowman, Blanche DuBois). A typical theatrical production involves the work of many behind-the-scenes people, from costume and set designers to stage managers and stagehands.

Standup performers, on the other hand, typically work alone. As a trainer, you have to take upon yourself many of the tasks assigned to the production crew in the theater:

- You have to be your own playwright. You have to create and develop your own character (your training persona), and you have to write your own script (training materials).

- You have to be your own director. You have to decide for yourself where to stand, when to sit, when to pause, how to deliver the material, where to set up, and how to use your "props." You also have to evaluate your own performance with a director's objective eye.

- You have to be your own set, lighting, and costume designer. You have to decide where to put such things as the overhead projector on your "stage"; you have to decide what lighting adjustments need to be made so that the trainees can see your transparencies; and you have to decide what to wear.

Standup trainers, thus, have total responsibility for their "act." The good news is that you don't have to worry about anyone else messing up your performance. The bad news is that you do have to worry about yourself messing up. This is why you need a protocol for preparation.

# Preparing for Your Standup Training

| Stages | Exercises |
|---|---|
| 1. Create and Develop Your Persona. | • Developing Your Persona (Internal Analysis)<br>• Developing Your Persona (External Analysis)<br>• Analyzing Your Role Model<br>• Creating Your Personal Press Release<br>• Analyzing Your Costume |
| 2. Create and Develop Your Material. | • Storytelling<br>• Developing Examples<br>• Analyzing Jokes<br>• Collecting Humorous Quotes |
| 3. Tailor Your Persona and Your Material to Your Audience. | • Tailoring Your Material |
| 4. Rehearse Your Performance. | • A Checklist for a Mind Rehearsal |
| 5. Revise and Edit Your Material and Your Persona. | • A Checklist for Continuous Improvement |

# Creating and Developing Your Training Persona

The word *persona* is theatrical in origin. In Latin, *persona* means the mask one wears or the role one plays on the stage. (The word person comes from the same root.) In modern usage, a *persona* is "the role one assumes or displays in public or society; one's public image or personality, as distinguished from the inner self" (*New American Heritage Dictionary*).

The advantage of creating a public persona is that it enables you to be objective when dealing with criticism (from yourself or from others). You don't have to take negative comments personally. (They just didn't like me.) You take them professionally. (They didn't like my persona.)

For trainers, this objectivity is extremely helpful because it allows you to adapt and modify your training style without feeling that somehow you've betrayed your "real" self. If your trainees comment negatively at the end of class on some aspect of your delivery (Instructor was too intense—made me nervous.), you don't have to slide into a slough of despond because you've been criticized. Rather, you can re-examine your training persona to see what adjustments can be made to soften the intensity.

A few years ago in a train-the-trainer class I was conducting, I videotaped a somewhat experienced technical trainer as he presented a short session on how to operate a widget-processing machine. The key point of his instruction was the need for careful attention to safety procedures.

The persona that this technical trainer was presenting was described (by myself as well as his fellow trainers) as "Mr. Know It All." His whole demeanor—how he stood, how he gestured, how he spoke—gave us the impression that he was "talking down" to us. For example, at one point he put one hand on his hip, wagged his finger at us, frowned, and said (in a most sarcastic tone), "If you put your hand in this part of the machine, that will definitely be *ungood*."

During playback, the technical trainer could see his own persona in action, and he agreed with our response. He worked on changing his stance and his gestures. He took the sarcasm out of his voice and smiled more. He transformed himself from "Mr. Know It All" to "Concerned and Caring Demonstrator."

If you can describe your training persona objectively, then you can also modify it to achieve different objectives. Perhaps "Mr. Know It All" might be an effective persona for a class of truly recalcitrant trainees who had been hurt on the job once too often because of carelessness and inattention to safety procedures. "Concerned and Caring Demonstrator" seems more suitable for a class of new recruits as yet unfamiliar with the hazards of the machinery.

There are as many training personas as there are individual personalities. To discover your own range of "characters," it is always helpful to start from where you are. How do you think you appear to others?

## Developing Your Persona

(Individual Exercise)

Write a description of your own personality. What sort of person are you? How do you think you come across to others? List adjectives and descriptive phrases that sum up who you think you are:

Next, videotape yourself. Do any of the descriptions you listed above change when you see yourself on tape? Are you surprised by anything you see?

Take a "reality check" to see if your own perceptions accurately match what others see in you:

Stand up in front of a group of 5 to 10 people who don't know you very well. Give each person a piece of paper, and ask them to write down any adjectives or descriptive phrases that occur to them as they watch and listen to you. Then conduct a mini training session on anything you're an expert in (e.g., how to tie shoelaces, how to bake a cake, or how to trim a moustache). Afterwards, collect all the slips of paper and analyze your audience's remarks, looking for patterns and similarities. Ignore any oddball comments. List others' perceptions of you here:

Compare the results of your individual and group analyses. Are you beginning to see a pattern developing? Do any of your own descriptions correspond to what others see? Do any differ?

## Analyzing Your Role Model                    (Individual Exercise)

It also can be helpful to decide which famous standup comedian you are most like. Then you can study this person and learn which kinds of material work best for your type. (I am going to worry about you if you pick Don Rickles. Make sure your role model is appropriate for a trainer.)

List any standup comics or performers whose public personas closely match your own:

After you have completed the previous exercises, you should be ready to finalize a description of your stage persona.

Many standup comics are booked at small comedy clubs based on the attraction of their promotional materials. Imagine that you get your training "gigs" the same way: You have to send the club owner (or training coordinator) a concise description of your act—who you are, what you are like on stage, other comedians (or trainers) to whom you could be compared. Write such a description of yourself below.

# Dress for Your Persona

When you're creating and developing your training persona, you also must consider what sort of a costume you're going to wear.

Stage actors know how important the right costume is. It would be difficult for an audience to believe in an actor playing, say, the part of Lady Bracknell in Oscar Wilde's *The Importance of Being Earnest* if she were to walk out on stage dressed in blue jeans and a T-shirt. Indeed, many actors find that the right costume is the key to completing their performance.

Even an actor who performs in a "modern dress" play will consider what he or she wears on stage to be an integral part of the performance. First impressions do count, which is why actors work very closely with the costume designer to create a "look" that an audience will respond to immediately.

Think about how your favorite standup comedians dress for their performances. Some adopt a relaxed, casual look (George Carlin, Paula Poundstone); some a more formal appearance (Jay Leno, Marsha Warfield). All have chosen costumes to complement their personas.

In his *Dress for Success* book, John Molloy concluded that business people who want to be successful have to achieve a certain professional "look": dark suit and tie for men, dark suit (with skirt, not pants) and a tie-like neck thing for women. (The humorist Dave Barry assumes this means that Molloy thinks women should dress like nuns.)

Yes it's true, there is a professional costume that trainers must wear if they wish to be taken seriously by others in the business world. (But I believe the costume allows for more variety and individuality than Molloy might have approved of.) The key is to choose what you wear based on what works for your persona and what will work for your audience.

Once I attended a professional training society program where the presenter—an experienced trainer—appeared "on stage" wearing a nicely tailored red suit, a sheer white blouse, and (can you believe this?) a red brassiere. (The reason we knew her bra was red, of course, is that we could see it!) Obviously, this trainer had decided to adopt the "Madonna Joins the Business World" persona—certainly fine if she were instructing a class of would-be cocktail waiters in the proper way to serve a martini, but hardly appropriate for a group of training professionals dressed for the most part like members of the clergy.

The bad examples abound: All costumed in conservative suits, a group of business professionals and I once sat through a training session on improving communication skills conducted by a cut-offs-and-T-shirt-clad trainer. "But the workshop was held on a *Saturday*," explained Mr. Anyone Here Ready for Volleyball and Beer. Here's another faux pas: For a training session on ISO 9000 Certification Procedures for upper-level managers, an extremely intelligent, eminently knowledgeable, highly educated, tiny and high-voiced Asiatic woman showed up in a pink dress with lace at the neck, bows at the waist, and ruffles on the sleeves. Needless to say, her "Rebecca of Sunnybrook Farm" persona didn't do much for her credibility.

These folks obviously didn't take the time to think about what costume would best suit their professional persona. The following exercises can help ensure that this oversight never happens to you.

## Analyzing Your Costume

Review your description of your persona, and decide what costume will work best for both your situation and your audience. As a standup trainer, you probably want to settle on a costume that can be described as "relaxed professional": formal enough to make you look credible to your trainees, but not so formal that you look like you're presiding at a state funeral.

Describe your training costume:

Some last tips on your standup trainer costume:

- Wear comfortable clothing. Tight pants, skirts, collars, or shoes are bound to produce an "up tight" performance. To appear relaxed in front of trainees, wear clothes that you can move in easily.

- Don't let your costume "upstage" your performance. The audience should leave the training session remembering what you taught them, not what you were wearing. Avoid flashy, clunky jewelry. Don't overpower the audience with bright colors. (A bright yellow suit might be all right for a 25-minute speech, but it might be nauseating for an all-day seminar.)

# Creating and Developing Your Material

We're talking standup material here, not training material. I assume you already have designed and developed the information you want to teach. What you need to do now is develop humorous, dramatic material that illustrates your training objectives. The classical Roman poet Horace once said that the greatest orators of his day knew how to "instruct and delight" their audiences. Assuming that you know what to say to instruct your audience, what can you say to delight them?

You can create your own material, or you can quote someone else. Or you can do both.

Best of all is to create your own material because then you can be sure that what you say will complement your established persona. When the story you tell, the analogy you present, or the example you give springs directly from your own perception of the world around you, your audience will respond positively. They will accept your point of view because what you say naturally will be backed up by how you say it.

## Tell Stories

The easiest way to add humor and/or drama to your training session is to tell a story about yourself or someone you know. Self-effacing humor can be very effective, because it helps your audience relate to you as a real human being who has had to overcome some of the same problems they are currently encountering.

For example, one story I tell about myself in my Presentation Strategies class concerns the time I walked on fire. In more detail than I will go into here (you have to see me do this in person to really appreciate the humor), I describe how I was invited to a fire-walking seminar; how I went just to check it out, not intending to actually walk on fire or anything; how I got caught up in the enthusiasm of the whole thing (it was the chanting that sent me over the edge); how I found myself barefoot in front of a pit filled with coals heated to a blistering 1500 degrees; how I chanted my way across the coals; how I was thrilled to discover that I had, indeed, walked on fire; how I felt at that moment that I could do anything, conquer any problem, reach any goal; how the next morning I discovered I could not walk at all because of the huge blisters on my feet; and how I lied to my doctor and told her that I had burned the bottoms of my feet when I "accidentally" knocked over a hot hibachi at a barbecue party.

The point of my story, I tell my trainees, is that, with faith, you can overcome any fear, even the fear of speaking in public. (The punch line of my story is that sometimes you also learn a useful lesson: You can't really walk on coals heated to 1500 degrees without burning the hell out of your feet.) True story. Just slightly elaborated for comic effect.

People you know are also a good source for comic material. I frequently use my son when I want to explain, in my Writing Basics class, how language constantly evolves. First I ask, "How many of you here have teenaged children?" A few hands go up. "How many of you here have ever been teenaged children?" A few more hands go up. "Every generation adds new words to the general vocabulary," I point out. "My son, for example, says his new shoes are *bad*. When did *bad* come to mean *good*?"

Or in my Writing Strategies class, I might illustrate how writer's block can inhibit anyone's productivity by relating the story of the time my son had to write a 600-word essay on "The Gerbil." "He started writing at 10 p.m. the night before the essay was due," I sigh. (All the parents in the class can relate to this.) "'The gerbil is a small, furry rodent,' he began. Then he stopped. 'One, two, three....' I knew we were in for a long night," I moan.

The opportunities for trainers to tell relevant stories are endless. Suppose you're an internal trainer conducting a new employee orientation program. You could tell a story about something humorous that happened to you the first day you started work at X Company. Or suppose you're a technical trainer conducting a class in proper soldering techniques. You could dramatically describe what happened to you when you became distracted and attempted to solder your own hand to the circuit board.

Put 10 trainers in a room together, and they'll probably come up with 100 different usable stories. I've gathered a few of my favorite stories, all guaranteed to get a laugh (or at least an amused chuckle) as well as provide you with the opportunity to *dramatize*. Feel free to use any of these as written, or adapt them to fit your own instructional design. (Embellish! Elaborate! That's what acting is all about!)

# Stories for Trainers

## Neil Armstrong and the Rabbit in the Moon

Not long after his historic step on to the surface of the moon, Neil Armstrong became a speaker on the international lecture circuit. One day he was in Japan telling the story of his lunar adventures (with an interpreter's help) to a group of school children. A small child asked Armstrong, "What was it really like on the moon?" Without thinking, Armstrong offhandedly replied, "Well it wasn't made of green cheese." The interpreter said in Japanese, "Well, I didn't see any rabbits."

You see, the interpreter had a translation problem. Unlike Americans, the Japanese have never heard of the expression, "The moon is made of green cheese." If he had interpreted exactly what Armstrong had said, the children would have stared at the speaker with that all-too-familiar blank look of incomprehension. I can imagine one studious child asking, "Did you go to the moon specifically to see green cheese?"

The translator decided to go for a metaphor instead of a literal translation. He knew that the Japanese have a folklore tradition of stories about a rabbit in the moon (similar to the United States' tradition of the man in the moon). The children, the interpreter knew, would be familiar with this reference, and Armstrong's meaning would be clear: Science has replaced folklore.

*Point of This Story:* To communicate effectively with others, whether in speaking or in writing, you must create meaning in others' minds. You must translate technical terminology or esoteric jargon in ways that your audience can understand and appreciate.

## The Man Who Died From Public Speaking

I frequently tell my Presentations Strategies students not to worry; no one has ever actually died from speaking in public. Then I pause, think again, and tell them, "Well, that's not exactly true."

In 1841, U.S. President William Henry Harrison delivered an inaugural speech lasting over two hours on a cold, blustery, January day in Washington, D.C. He caught pneumonia and died one month later.

*Point of This Story:* Public speaking won't kill you. But speaking too long might.

## Don't Ask Me What I Think of You

A respected drama critic accepted the invitation to opening night of a young writer's new play. He attended, but slept through the entire performance.

The playwright was extremely upset. He asked, "How could you sleep when you knew how much I valued your opinion?"

"My dear young man," the critic responded. "Sleep is an opinion."

*Point of This Story:* There are no boring subjects, only boring trainers.

## Which Came First—the Rock or the Hard Place?

One night at sea, a ship's captain saw what looked like the lights of another ship heading toward him. He had his signaler blink to the other ship:

"Change your course 10 degrees south."

The reply came back: "Change your course 10 degrees north."

The ship's captain answered: "I am a captain. Change your course south."

To which the reply was, "Well I am a seaman first-class. Change your course north."

This infuriated the captain, so he signaled back: "Dammit, I say change your course south. I'm on a battleship!"

To which the reply came back: "And I say change your course north. I'm in a lighthouse!"

*Point of This Story:* Don't shoot your mouth off before you know all the facts.

## How To Justify Your Consultant Fee

Charles Steinmetz, the famous German-American electrical engineer and inventor, was known as the "Electrical Wizard" during his long career at the company General Electric. After he retired, GE brought him back as a consultant to determine what had caused a breakdown in a complex system of machines. The cause of the breakdown baffled all of GE's experts.

Steinmetz spent some time walking around and testing the various parts of the machine complex. Finally, he took a piece of chalk out of his pocket and marked an "X" on a particular part of one machine.

The GE people disassembled the machine, discovering to their amazement that the defect lay precisely where Steinmetz's chalk mark was located.

Some days later, Steinmetz sent GE an invoice for $10,000. The company protested the amount and asked that he itemize the expenses. He sent back an itemized invoice:

> Making one chalk mark . . . . . . . . . . . . . . $1.00
> Knowing where to place it. . . . . . . . $9,999.00

*Point of This Story:* What is knowledge worth?

## One in a Million

One summer morning, a young boy walking on a beach found thousands upon thousands of starfish beached with the low tide. He stood on the beach and threw them back into the water—one at a time—so they wouldn't die.

An old man came up to him and caustically said, "Kid, what do you think you're doing? You can't possibly get even a fraction of these starfish in the water before they die! What possible difference is all your work going to make?"

"Well sir," the boy replied as he leaned down, grabbed another starfish, and threw it back into the ocean, "it makes all the difference in the world to that one."

*Point of This Story:* Little things do count.

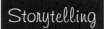 

(Individual Exercise)

Pick any point you want to make in your training session, and select a personal story to illustrate it. Then either write the story in the space below or, better yet, tell a friend or a group of people. Ask whomever you tell for feedback. (Even better, videotape yourself telling the story, so you can critique your delivery, too.)

# Train With Examples

Do you want some magic words to liven up your training sessions? Here they are: "For example...."

We trainers are always trying to show how theory can be put into practice. In fact, this "real-world applications" approach is the distinguishing characteristic that makes us trainers, not just teachers. We present the theory: "A well-organized document is an effective communication tool." Then we say the magic words: "For example, look at this document on the overhead. Do you think it's well organized?" We use specifics to illustrate generalizations.

Standup comics do precisely the same thing. They set up a comic bit with a generalization and then punch in a specific example. For example (I'm practicing what I'm preaching here), in a routine he presented early in his career, George Carlin generalized about how the laid-back 1960s had quite an impact on the educational output of high school students. Then he got specific: "In one semester, students in shop class went from making zip guns to hash pipes."

Generalizations by themselves are boring. They create no pictures in the listeners' minds. But zip guns to hash pipes? Wow! Everyone can see those students in shop class.

It's easy to add lively examples to your presentation. Just think of a point you want to make and say the magic words. For example (I'm doing it again), in my writing classes I frequently point out that politically correct labels are fine to a certain extent. But we must be careful about taking things too far. (Now there's a generalization for you. Doesn't it just cry out for the magic words?) "For example," I say, "I have a friend who thinks he's too short. He describes himself as 'vertically challenged.'"

In my grammar class, I point out that punctuation rules are not merely fiendish devices invented by Miss Thistlebottom to drive writers insane. In many cases, marks of punctuation can seriously affect the meaning of a sentence. Here is an example (cited in the book *Questions You Always Wanted To Ask About English But Were Afraid To Raise Your Hand*):

> Which sentence may result in an embarrassing situation?
>
> a) The butler was asked to stand by the door and call the guests' names as they arrived.
>
> b) The butler was asked to stand by the door and call the guests names as they arrived.

An example also can be an analogy. I frequently point out that a writer who starts writing without a plan or an outline is like an architect who decides to build a house without a blueprint. "I hate blueprints," the architect sniffs. "They inhibit my creativity. So we're just going to get a bunch of trucks, fill them with building materials—bricks, boards, conduit and wiring, etc.—and go to the site you've picked for your house and just start building."

Now one of two things might happen. You might indeed end up with a house that's a work of art—even featured on the cover of *Architectural Digest*. You also might end up with a house with no bathrooms. (Ooops!) The point is that blueprints and plans allow you to make changes and predict success before you start working! That's why writers need blueprints too.

## Developing Examples

See for yourself how easy it is to add specific, humorous examples. List one or two points you wish to make in your next training session, and create as many specific examples as you can think of:

# Analyze Jokes Carefully

Of all the different types of humorous material, stories and examples are the easiest to write for yourself. The most difficult to create are jokes. Obviously some people are very good at this, and they actually make a living as "joke writers" for famous comedians and talk-show hosts. I am not one of these people. (If you are good at creating jokes, or just want to learn more about how to write them, I recommend Gene Perret's book, *Comedy Writing Step by Step*.)

Jokes tend to exist as ends in themselves. The point is the punch line. Stories, conversely, are the means to an instructional end. They illustrate a point in a humorous way. If your joke doesn't get a laugh, it's a bomb. If your story doesn't get a laugh, it's still education. There's a lot less pressure involved when you devise stories or examples for a training session, so you'll probably be much more creative (and productive).

Additionally, because jokes are written as ends in themselves, you take a chance when you tell one in a training session that your joke make be either irrelevant or (worst of all) inappropriate. Jokes are inappropriate when they make fun of people unfairly, or touch on subjects that should be taboo in a professional setting (sex, religion, politics). Here's an example of a (probably) irrelevant joke:

> A gorilla goes into a bar and orders a dry martini, on the rocks, with a twist. The bartender is shocked at first to see a gorilla ordering a drink, but he figures he'll take advantage of the situation. So he fixes the gorilla the drink, serves it to him, and says, "That'll be $25 dollars." The gorilla gives him the money and sips his drink. The bartender then says, "You know, we don't get many gorillas in here." The gorilla replies, "Well at $25 dollars a drink, I can understand why."

Did you think that was funny? Did it make you laugh? (Most people I tell it to just groan.) Most important, how in the world could this joke ever illustrate anything being taught in a training session? Tell this joke in your next class and you might get a chuckle (I doubt it), but you certainly won't achieve any educational objective.

Of course, not all jokes fall into the irrelevant and/or offensive categories. Here's one I told during a training session in communication skills for a group of Air Force testing-and-evaluation personnel (military and civilian). My point was that to be effective communicators in the 21st century, we will need to be well-organized. To write or speak in an organized fashion, we will need a protocol, a plan. It's not enough that we can get the information to people more quickly than ever with faxes and modems. The message must still make sense when it gets there.

> "This situation reminds me," I told my Air Force audience, "of the Air Force fighter-pilot who radioed the control tower: 'The good news is that I'm making excellent time. The bad news is I'm lost.'"

My audience laughed heartily at this. (Although I must point out here that the stories and examples I used all got much bigger laughs than this joke.)

A somewhat risky but perhaps worth-the-risk joke-telling technique involves tailoring an old ethnic joke to poke fun at some group your audience is currently worried about or frustrated with. Suppose that your trainees have recently been experiencing some trying times with some hard-headed and demanding government regulatory auditors. Simply redirect their hostility by changing the offensive and tiresome, "How many [ethnic group] does it take to change a light bulb?" (Answer: Six. One to hold the bulb and five to turn the chair.) If you're teaching a class in Change Management, you might ask your trainees, "How many *corporate vice-presidents* does it take to change a light bulb?" (Answer: Six. One to change the bulb and five to sit around and talk about how much better it was before the change.)

Choose a joke you have written yourself (or one that you have heard). Then ask yourself the following questions:

1.  How is the joke relevant to any of my training objectives? What point in my presentation does this joke illustrate?

2.  Could this joke be considered in any way offensive to any member of my audience?

If you answer "no" to the first question, don't use the joke. If you answer "yes" to the second question, don't use the joke. When in doubt, throw it out.

# Collect Quotes

I mentioned earlier that the best humorous material comes from your own experiences: things that have actually happened to you or to people you know. You also can supplement this material with bits and routines borrowed from others; just remember to always give credit where credit is due.

Quotations from well-known people can be a fruitful source of humorous material to supplement any training session. One of my favorite quotable authors is humorist Fran Leibowitz. When I want to make the point in my communication skills classes that precision in communication is not always desirable, I mention that Fran Leibowitz wonders why the airlines are always so hung up on precise arrival and departure times. Flight schedules persistently announce that planes will depart at 9:57 and arrive at 12:48. "Have you ever heard of a plane actually departing and arriving at such a specific time?" Leibowitz wonders. "If the airlines are going to be realistic, they should announce, 'Flight 365 departing Atlanta at 9:00 or 9:30, arriving New York 12ish.'"

In my writing class, I illustrate what I mean about clarity in writing by quoting Mark Twain. I remind my class that the author of *Huckleberry Finn* was also a free-lance writer: He got paid by the word for many of his shorter works. "I never write metropolis for seven cents," Twain once remarked, "when I can get the same amount for city." This quote always gets a hearty laugh (and it drives home the point, too).

# Some Quotable Quotes for Trainers

I've loosely categorized some of the quotes that I use to illustrate a variety of training objectives. (If you'd like to share yours, please feel free to send them to me as well.)

### Communications Skills

A police officer once told me that he became a cop because he "wanted a job in which the customer was always wrong."

"All people who make generalizations are fools." —*Anonymous*

"Speak when you're angry, and you'll make the best speech you'll ever regret."
—*Time* magazine

---

"Half the world is composed of people who have something to say and can't: The other half is composed of people who have nothing to say and keep on saying it."
                                                                    —*Robert Frost*

"The opposite of talking isn't listening. The opposite of talking is waiting."
                                                                    —*Fran Leibowitz*

Here is Fran Leibowitz's rendition of the "complete and unabridged record of conversation of the general public since time immemorial:"

> a. Hi, how are you?
> b. I did not.
> c. Good. Now you know how I feel.
> d. Do you mind if I go ahead of you? I only have one thing.

"I wish people who have trouble communicating would just shut up."
                                                                    —*Tom Lehrer*

Humorist Dave Barry has announced that this year the IRS has established a helpful, toll-free number for taxpayers. The number is 1-800-AUDIT-ME.

"I've come to this conclusion.
         It's one I've long supposed:
The boss's door is open—
         It's his mind that's closed."
                                                                    —*Robert Orben*

## Building Confidence/Achieving Success

"Confidence is going after Moby Dick with a longboat, a harpoon, and a jar of tartar sauce."
                                                                    —*Anonymous*

"Don't be afraid to take a big step if one is indicated. You can't cross a chasm in two small jumps."
                                                                    —*David Lloyd George*

"If you aren't fired with enthusiasm, you will be fired with enthusiasm."
                                                                    —*Vince Lombardi*

"If you can't win, make the fellow ahead of you break the record."
                                                                    —*Anonymous*

## Public Speaking Skills

Here's the comedy group Second City's producer Joseph Keefe's advice for improving your eye contact with your audience: "Always avoid letting your eyes make contact with each other."

The secret to successful public speaking is just what your mother always told you: "Stand up straight, look people in the eye, and stop fidgeting!"

"It takes me three weeks to prepare a good impromptu speech."

—*Mark Twain*

On overcoming stage fright: "It will be all right when what you have to say is more important than the fact that your knees are knocking."

—*Eleanor Roosevelt*

"There are fewer [more pleasant] times in life than when you're finished speaking."

—*Andy Rooney*

"A speech is like a love affair: Anyone can start it, but to end it requires considerable skill."

—*Lord Mancroft*

## Stress and Control

"The leading cause of stress is reality. What is reality but a collective hunch?"

—*Jane Wagner*

"Stressed spelled backwards is desserts. Does anyone else find that meaningful?"

—*Ellen Dowling*

## Collecting Humorous Quotes

(Individual Exercise)

Develop a "clipping file" for humorous quotes from well-known people. You can browse through the many collections of quotations on the market to get you started. Two good examples of such collections are *The 637 Best Things Anybody Ever Said,* edited by Robert Byrne, and *The Portable Curmudgeon*, edited by John Winokur.

Remember to always credit the source of quotations and to apply the joke-analysis test: Is the quotation relevant to a specific training objective, and is it appropriate for the training audience?

# Tailoring Your Persona and Material to the Audience

*I give the same mashed potatoes for each speech.*
*I just change the gravy.*

—Dr. Norman Vincent Peale

## Tailor Your Persona

The persona you described earlier will serve you well in most training situations. Minor adjustments, however, may need to be made for certain atypical occurrences. For example, a lively, energetic persona helps to keep lower-level employees alert and interested through eight or so hours of skills training. If you are then called upon to conduct a shorter workshop for upper management, you may find your highly charged style to be a bit of a turn-off.

Take your cue from your audience: Add entertaining anecdotes and participatory exercises for staff members and first-line supervisors who will appreciate your humor. Jettison most of the funny stuff, eschew the exercises, and get to the point for senior-managers and vice-presidents who will not want you to waste their time.

The same point holds true for your trainer's costume. A more informal look (sport coat and jacket or brightly colored coordinates) will work nicely for staff and supervisors. Dress more formally (and conservatively) for the big brass.

## Tailor Your Material

Any humorous material you use must always be tailored to your specific audience to be truly effective. Trainers are supposed to know all about the importance of tailoring, since they train so many different types of people with differing backgrounds, differing educational levels, and differing interests. Yet I have seen supposedly experienced and successful training professionals ignore this basic courtesy. They deliver a "canned" presentation, making no specific reference whatsoever to the people who are actually in the room.

I once was present at a luncheon during a society conference for professional trainers. The luncheon speaker was a trainer with many credentials in the profession and the society. After about 15 minutes into his presentation, I realized that the speaker had not even mentioned the word trainer, nor had he given any indication that he was speaking to an audience of trainers. It occurred to me that if we could have frozen the speaker in time for a moment, cleared all the trainers out of the room, replaced them with, say, atomic physicists, then unfrozen the moment, he would have continued on with his same presentation. His material was obviously more important than his audience.

To tailor your material to your audience, just do what the best standup comics do when they play local comedy clubs. They do their homework. They learn about the city in which they'll be performing, and then they insert local references into their prepared material. Audiences love this. Besides, a local reference personalizes the comic material, makes it relevant, and always gets a better response than generic material. For example, comics visiting a club in Albuquerque, New Mexico, might have a joke in their routine that begins, "A guy goes into a bar." It's guaranteed that this joke, whatever its punch line, will get a bigger laugh if the comic begins, "A guy goes into a bar on East Central Avenue." An Albuquerque audience will recognize and respond to the local reference instantly.

You should also learn the "language" of your trainees in order to tailor your material to them. (If you are an internal trainer, you should be able to do this quite easily. In fact, this ability to speak the same language is a basic advantage internal trainers have over external trainers.) If you're training, say, people in the semiconductor industry, sprinkle your material with references to chips and wafers, microprocessors, and clean rooms. If you're training people in the health-care industry, include patients, physicians, bedside manners, and bedpans. If you're training people in law enforcement, collect all the lawyer jokes you can think of. (Police officers love lawyer jokes. I wonder why?)

If you're planning to train a group of people in an industry unfamiliar to you, do some research. Talk to people who know the language, and ask them to give you some key vocabulary words and identify any current concerns your audience might have. Better yet, interview your trainees in person or by phone, before your training session. You'll get lots of ideas for material to personalize your training objectives.

## Tailoring Your Material                    (Individual Exercise)

Look back over any of the material you've considered previously.
Choose one or two "bits" (stories, examples, jokes, quotations), and
devise several different ways to tailor them to fit a variety of audiences.

# Rehearsing Your Performance

## Rehearse Before a "Real" Audience

I personally have never found it particularly helpful to rehearse before a "mock" audience (my mother, my spouse, my friends, or anyone else I can rope into pretending to be my real audience). First of all, a pretend audience will never be the same as a real audience; your family will never give you the same response as your real trainees.

You could try rehearsing before an audience of your peers (other trainers). But just remember that other trainers will have a tendency to evaluate you on your delivery style alone; they may not be able to comment on whether or not you taught them anything.

A truly effective rehearsal is a "pilot" program. Assemble a volunteer group of real trainees and try out your material on them. Best of all, videotape yourself during the pilot.

## Check Your Timing

A major concern for both standup comics and trainers is the timing of their performance. Standup comics are usually given a set amount of time to perform (six minutes to an hour), and a rehearsal of some sort to give them a rough idea of how much material they can include in their allotted time. I say a "rough" idea because the audience always has the power to throw the comic's timing off by laughing uproariously (and lengthily) at a certain joke or by staring stonily into space. The comic might wind up cutting jokes from the act if time runs short, or inserting additional material if things move along more quickly than planned.

Likewise, trainers should use a pilot rehearsal to get a rough sense of timing. Do you have too much material for one day? Not enough? Did that particular exercise take twice as long as you anticipated? Your pilot audience can give you useful feedback, but remember that each audience will respond differently to your material, so your timing will vary to some extent each time you present.

# Anticipate Your Audience

What I have found most useful in preparing for a training session is what I call a "mind rehearsal." As I go over my training materials, I estimate how much time I'll need for each section, each page of the training manual, or each activity. I picture my trainees, think about their particular situation, and try to imagine how they might respond to any given part of my presentation. Then I prepare "backup" material: If the audience zooms through this activity, I'll include this other activity. If the audience responds very positively to this section, I'll include a longer debriefing. If the audience doesn't seem to be getting it, I'll plan for several alternate examples or anecdotes to make the point clearer.

If you're sitting in the audience at a comedy club, you never know what material the comic may have decided to leave out or insert at the last moment. If you're attending a training session, you don't always know what modifications to the schedule the trainer is making in response to time constraints.

The best thing about a mind rehearsal is that it calms you down, focuses your attention on the audience (instead of yourself), and sets the stage for spontaneous, but personalized, ad-libs. You can conduct a mind rehearsal in your office as you prepare your materials, in your car on the way to the training session, or in the actual training space as your wait for the trainees to arrive.

❑ **Who is attending the presentation?** What kind of people will you be speaking to (e.g., salespeople, middle-managers, accountants)? Is the audience homogeneous or mixed? What concerns do they have?

❑ **Why are the trainees attending?** Have they been told to attend, or do they want to participate? (The answer to this question will determine how much motivation the audience will need.)

❑ **What do the trainees already know about the subject?** Are they totally unaware or misinformed? Do you need to start from ground-zero, or do the participants already have a basic understanding that only warrants further clarification?

❑ **What "language" will the trainees understand?** Are they familiar with computer or financial jargon? Management concepts? Engineering terminology? If they do not speak the language associated with the training topic, what translations will you need to make for them? For example, can you assume that participants in a computer training session will understand the comment "boot the DOS?" Or do you need to say "get the computer up and running"?

❑ **What do the trainees want to learn from the presentation?** All good speakers establish clear presentation objectives. But it's also important to consider what the audience's objectives are. If these objectives are different from yours, you have a problem to solve before the presentation.

❑ **How will the trainees respond to your objectives?** Will they be friendly and open-minded or resistant and skeptical? Perhaps they may even be hostile. (Wouldn't you rather know this before the actual presentation?)

❑ **What does the audience know about you?** Have you already established your credibility with them, or will you need to establish this in the first few moments of the presentation? Will the audience perceive you as a friend or foe? (The answer to this will determine your opening comments.)

# Revising and Adjusting Your Material and Your Persona

Stage actors, standup comics, and trainers all strive for perfection: that one perfect performance when everything works, when the audience responds exactly as they should, and when the universe itself shimmers with the brilliance of our presentation. Yeah, right. It may never happen, but it's worth shooting for anyway.

No stage actor is ever completely satisfied with his or her performance. Sure, Act Two was outstanding, but don't you think the pacing was a little slow in the first scene? No standup comic ever gets a huge laugh on every single joke. Sure, they loved the bit about the talking Coke machine, but why didn't they laugh at the snake joke? I love that joke!

So perhaps the journey here is, indeed, more important than the final destination. Continuous improvement is the name of the game, and it's the same for actors and comics as well as trainers. There's always something that could be improved, something that could be presented better.

Stage actors get their feedback during rehearsal from their director, or sometimes from an audience invited to see a dress rehearsal. On Broadway, a production goes through several weeks of "preview" performances before the official opening (when the critics attend). Many times, a production bound for Broadway is first premiered in another city (e.g., Washington, D.C. or Los Angeles). Before the production is finalized, it goes through many changes: scenes are added or dropped, lines are rewritten, staging is re-staged. Even after the play has been officially mounted, minor adjustments will continue to be made.

As a standup trainer working essentially alone, you will have to be your own best judge of what adjustments need to be made to your performance. Certainly you should use the feedback received from the participants attending your pilot presentation. Additionally, if you've used the mind-rehearsal technique for preparation, you'll want to review the following checklist to assess what changes should be made in your persona and your material.

Review the videotape of your pilot program and answer the following questions:

❑ How did the participants react to my persona? Was I too energetic? Too laid-back?

❑ How did the participants react to my costume? Was I dressed too formally? Too informally?

❑ How did the participants react to my comic material? Were the stories I told appropriate and relevant? Did I wander too far from my point? Did I offend anyone in the group?

❑ How was my timing? Did I finish earlier than I planned? Did I run over the specified time?

❑ Did my persona, costume, and my supplemental comic bits help the trainees learn?

Review these questions every time you train. That's why it's called continuous improvement. What works for one audience will often not work for another. What's funny and appropriate for one group may be boring or offensive to another. For example, a younger group of trainees may prefer your high energy style; an older, more traditionally-schooled group may prefer a more formal, less participatory style.

So how do you know when you've got it right? That's tricky to answer. I asked Sam Cox, Comedy Gym Workshop coach, how many times a joke had to bomb before the comic should give it up and throw it out. At least three times, he thought, with three different audiences. But don't you just know that if you took a chance and tried it just one more time on audience number four that same joke would get a huge laugh? That's probably why no comic tells just one joke; they tell 20 or 50. They go with the odds. All you have to do is be funny most of the time.

The same is true for trainers. In an eight-hour seminar, you don't have to make them laugh every time, just some of the time. In between, you're supposed to be teaching them something.

# Act Two: Polishing Your Technique

# Objective

In Act One, you learned how to develop funny stuff to supplement your serious training objectives. But as every comic knows, the key to a successful standup performance is not the ability to tell a funny story; it's the ability to tell a story funny. This Act shows how to do just that.

To be effective joke-tellers or humorous storytellers, trainers need to employ the same skills that actors use to portray a character on the stage: They must project their voices effectively; control their body movements, gestures, and facial expressions; concentrate and stay focused. The trainer who combines the stage actor's dramatization abilities with the humorous, slightly askew point of view of the standup comic will have little difficulty adding effective, appropriate humor to enliven any training session.

Welcome to Acting 101 for Trainers. This section presents some of the tricks and techniques that stage actors use to improve their vocal delivery, enhance their body movement, and remain focused in the midst of unforeseen distractions. I also have included numerous acting class exercises. Some can be done alone, while others require a group effort from several theatrically like-minded trainers.

Warning: You may not be able to see a direct link to training for every one of the points I make in this section. When actors take acting classes, they participate in exercises to develop their acting instruments—in other words, their bodies. They don't necessarily prepare for any particular role. The presumption is that a well-conditioned body, keen focus, sharp reflexes, graceful and purposeful gestures, an animated face, and a flexible, creative voice are useful to any role an actor might play on the stage.

I'm following the same presumption for trainers. If you practice the skills in this section, you will enhance your overall training delivery effectiveness. You will feel more comfortable in front of any group of trainees, you will be a more interesting storyteller, and you will be more mentally flexible and ready to deal with any unforeseen training problems. We're talking big picture here.

I also want to stress that playing theater games serves a dual purpose: The first is always to have fun; the second is to discover something about yourself. Thus, I have included exercises that, in the words of Clive Barker (*Theatre Games*), are designed to "reveal to the actors [or trainers] what happens when they work, and to help them be aware of the mind/body processes involved in their work… . One should never try to make an exercise or game work; one should set it up and let it take place."

If you're ready to play, read on.

# Improving Your Vocal Delivery

## Speak Up!

*The first rule which an actor must observe is that
of making oneself heard and understood. In fact,
this is not a rule, it is a matter of elementary
politeness, and failure to conform to it is an insult
to the spectator.*

—Jean-Louis Barrault
from *Actors on Acting*

The word *audience* comes from the Latin *audire,* meaning "to hear." In most theatrical productions (except for those taking place in large auditoriums with more than 2,000 seats), the actors do not use microphones. Rather, they must depend upon years of vocal training to reach the ears of those in the farthest seats. Even during a quiet love scene, the actors must be heard, not just seen.

I once went to a production of Tennessee Williams' "Cat on a Hot Tin Roof," performed by a university group in a 500-seat theater. The young acting students obviously were not accustomed to performing in such a large space and did not speak loudly enough to be heard by those of us seated at the back of the hall. As the play went on, those of us in the back began to shift forward in our seats, straining to hear what was being said on stage. Finally, one fed-up gentleman seated near me could stand it no longer: "Louder!" he shouted. The performers on stage, noticeably startled, immediately raised the volume, but only for a few moments. Gradually, they slipped back to their original muffled tones. "Louder!" the man yelled again. The rattled actors gamely attempted to comply, but soon resumed their quiet mumbling. At this point, the irritated critic decided that vocal coaching was a hopeless cause, and he left the theater. A steady stream of equally frustrated "auditors" followed him.

Training session participants also must be able to hear you comfortably, or they soon lose interest in your session's objectives. Most trainers don't conduct seminars in 2,000-seat auditoriums, and if they do, they most certainly would use a microphone. (By the way, if you know you are going to be "miked" during a training session, there are two things you must do: Get to the training

---

site early for a sound check, and request a wireless mike so you don't have to worry about handling it during the presentation.)

Typically, trainers conduct sessions in rooms that hold 20 to 30 people. The small size of the room may make some trainers complacent or may cause them to assume they can just speak normally and still be heard. But even in small rooms the sound can be deadened by poor acoustics or a particularly noisy group in the room next door. A participant in a training seminar should never have to say to the trainer, "Could you please speak up? We can't hear you back here."

The key is not merely to speak louder or to shout to be heard. Trained actors know that yelling is not the way to be heard in the theater. If you yell, your voice will be strident and unpleasant to the ear. Actors also know that shouting damages their voice quickly and leads to hoarseness. An actor may be playing a role that requires her to be on stage for two or more hours. If she shouts on stage for two hours, she will have no voice left for the next performance.

This dilemma is even worse for trainers since they frequently must speak to their audiences for eight hours, or two days, or even five days, depending on the length of the training session. A trainer who shouts to be heard is going to have a very short career.

Actors do not shout to be heard; they project their voices. Through intensive vocal training, they learn to speak from their diaphragms and use their entire chest area to support their voices. They spend countless hours learning how to control their breath and to direct the sound so that even a whisper can be heard by those in the back seats.

Complete this exercise in order to discover the difference between shouting and projecting. First try shouting. Shout out anything— perhaps your name, a quote, or a nonsensical phrase. Turn on a tape recorder so you can hear yourself. Play back the shouting and listen to yourself. Do you sound strident? Does your voice sound forced? Too high-pitched?

Next, put your hands on your diaphragm (the area of your chest just under your breast bone). Now whisper the same phrase you shouted earlier. Whisper as loudly as you can and feel what happens to your diaphragm as you do. Did you feel it tighten? You've just discovered your diaphragm.

Now tighten your diaphragm without saying anything. Keep your hands over it so you can feel it tighten. Relax. Tighten again. Relax. Now consciously tighten your diaphragm and speak the same phrase you shouted earlier. Play back your recorded voice. Does it sound louder? Stronger? More resonant?

If you practice consciously tightening your diaphragm when speaking, you will notice a gradual improvement in your vocal projection capabilities. It won't happen overnight, but you can improve your delivery and overcome any "breathy" qualities in your voice with practice.

Here's another vocal projection exercise that you can do alone. As you drive in your car, turn on the radio or tape player. Consciously tighten your diaphragm and sing along with your favorite songs. Don't just hum or mouth the words—SING! Belt it out! It doesn't matter whether or not you can carry a tune. You're in your car. Who's going to hear you? Practice this exercise religiously and eventually you'll hear the difference in your speaking voice.

## Projecting Your Voice

You need a partner for this exercise. Pick something to read or recite. Then stand 10 feet away from your partner and speak. Ask your partner how you sounded. Could you be heard clearly? Then stand 50 feet away from your partner and speak again. How was your volume this time? Then try the same thing at 100 feet. Any problems? Rely on your partner to tell you when your voice sounds confident and strong and when it sounds strident and forced.

By the way, you also can use this exercise when you begin a training session, especially in a fairly large room. If you think people in the back of the room might have problems hearing you, just pick out the person who's farthest away from you and ask, "Can you hear me all right back there?" If that person nods yes, you can be sure that the rest of the audience can hear you as well. You also can make arrangements ahead of time with an audience member who's seated in the back of the room to signal you if your voice begins to drop too low during any part of the session.

(Group Exercise)

In groups, improvise the following situations—all of which require you to call to each other across a wide distance. Remember to focus on projecting, not shouting.

❑ A guide and tourists are lost in a dark cave. The tourists have become separated from the guide.

❑ Mountain climbers, attached to each other by a rope, are climbing a high mountain in a blizzard.

❑ Parents standing on the front porch are calling out final instructions to teenagers in a car with the motor running.

❑ Patients in a hospital are trying to call a nurse in the hall without waking the other patients.

# Add Vocal Variety

What good is it if the your trainees can hear every word you say but you speak in a monotone? Vocal projection without vocal variety is no good. ("I had no trouble hearing the trainer, but, boy, was she boring to listen to!") A trainer who projects well but speaks in a monotone probably will have difficulty conveying the learning objectives to the trainees. (There is no greater deterrent to learning than listening to a monotonous trainer drone on, especially at 3:00 in the afternoon in a stuffy room after a heavy lunch.)

Variety is the spice of vocal delivery. Actors who can modulate their vocal pitch, vary their phrasing, alter their tone, and pause for dramatic effect are sure to keep their audiences entertained. Trainers who can do the same are sure to keep their audiences awake.

I recently observed a technical trainer conducting a session on something like, How To Connect Two Wires Together Without Electrocuting Yourself. A serious subject, indeed, and certainly an important on-the-job skill for trainees to learn. This could have been a dry, dull presentation that put people to sleep and caused them to forget the very safety procedures they were being taught. Instead, the instructor dramatized the consequences of inattention to hazardous wires by grasping two imaginary wires, touching them to each other, and then gasping in an eerie, pulsating voice (eyes bulging and body shaking), "Y-o-o-u-u d-d-o-o-n't want-t-t to-o-o d-d-o-o th-th-is!" The trainees laughed, and they got the point. (I suspect they would certainly remember the trainer's performance if they were ever tempted to connect the wrong wires!)

How do you know how much variety you can add to your vocal delivery unless you explore your own vocal abilities? The following exercises offer opportunities to explore just what you're capable of doing with your own voice.

## Adding Vocal Variety

To add variety to your vocal delivery, you need to discover your range of "voices." Anyone can learn to be a decent mimic—you just have to listen carefully and practice. In your car, consciously mimic the voices you hear on the radio. At home, get out your tape recorder and listen to yourself as you practice a range of voices. You'll be amazed at how much variety you can add to your vocal delivery just by conscious practice and attentive listening.

Here are some voices for you to try. Speak as though you were

- a record being played at 16 rpm (very slowly, with a deep voice)
- a record being played at 45 rpm (very quickly, like a Munchkin)
- out of breath
- drunk
- suffering from a terrible cold
- laughing hysterically
- crying hysterically
- in terrible pain
- the Star Trek computer
- very frightened
- very embarrassed
- very angry
- someone with marbles in your mouth
- an opera singer
- extremely bored
- extremely interested

If you want to practice articulation, try some good old tongue-twisters:

- Which witch tooted the flute.
- Peter placed plain plums on plaid plastic.
- Freshly fried flying fish.
- The Smith youth's tooth was underneath.
- Tom threw Tim three thumbtacks.
- The sixth Sheik's sixth sheep is sick.

Stage actors know that it's not the lines themselves that convey meaning to the audience: It's the subtext, or way the actors say the lines, that tells the audience what the character really feels. A fun way for trainers to develop a facility for subtext is to play the Jack and Jill game:

The trainers/trainees are divided into groups. Each group acts out this situation: Two people are driving a car that suddenly breaks down in the middle of the street. Two police officers offer assistance. The car is fixed, and they all go on their way. The rule is that all players must use only the words "Jack and Jill" when they speak.

This exercise is called the Dubbing game:

Participants break out into groups of four. Two players represent actors in a foreign film, and two players represent their dubbed voices. The players who are the actors go on stage and begin to work through a simple improvisation (e.g., a mother punishing her child for taking cookies). Announce the situation so all players can hear. The dubbing players then provide all the speech for the actors, who just move their mouths silently.

# Control Your Speed

Some trainers speak too slowly. Some speak too quickly. If you are a member of the slow group, you run the risk of boring your trainees. If you are a vocal speed freak (I personally have been known to fall into this category), you may end up leaving your trainees far behind.

Video and audiotaping are critical here. You need to hear yourself speak during an actual training session. It will do you little good to tape yourself reading a piece of prose. Nearly everyone speaks at an appropriate speed when they're conscious of what they're doing.

You need to hear and see how you speak when you're not concentrating on the speed of your delivery. For example, you need to hear yourself speak during the first five minutes or so of your class, when you're most energized, most nervous, most "wired." If you have any pacing problems, this is where you'll need to consciously speed up or slow down.

Normal speaking speed is 125 to 175 words per minute. Tape yourself, time yourself, and then (the next time you present) consciously slow down or speed up.

# Overcome Other Vocal Problems

For some trainers, volume and variety are not the only aspects of vocalization that need to be improved. A trainer may have too high-pitched a voice. (This can be particularly true for women.) Another may have too nasal a voice or an accent that is difficult for trainees to understand.

Such serious vocal problems cannot be "cured" overnight. To begin working on a particular problem with vocalization, I recommend reading Cicely Berry's *Voice and the Actor,* and practicing the multitude of exercises she provides for developing a pleasant-sounding voice. (Practice with a tape recorder so that you can hear your voice, determine what to work on, and monitor your progress.)

Your best bet is to find a competent vocal coach and prepare for months, perhaps longer, of serious practice and coaching. Do not despair! With time and tenacity, the most irritating, whiny, impossible to understand voice can be trained to sound like Peter Jennings's or Connie Chung's. Actors go through years of vocal training to develop a "standard" accent, which then allows them to take on a variety of dialects as their parts require. Laurence Olivier worked for months with a vocal coach to lower his natural speaking range so that he could portray Othello convincingly. Margaret Thatcher used a vocal coach from the National Theatre to help her lower her naturally high pitch.

The untrained trainer's voice can distract trainees, or put them to sleep. Conversely, a trained trainer's voice can stimulate trainees' attention and help them remember what they've learned.

## Scene 2

# Learning To Move

> *...voice and speech, the soul and the mind, are not separate from the body but originate from it, emanate through it. Therefore, if the body is inert, unmotivated, and artificially positioned, the soul will also be deadened, the mind will freeze up, thoughts will become occupied with external irrelevancies, the throat will tighten, and we will produce mechanical or unintelligible words.*
>
> —Uta Hagen, *A Challenge for the Actor*

## Warm Up and Calm Down

Trainers have many opportunities throughout a typical training session to move around the training room. You may start out by standing next to a table on which you've placed your notes and an overhead projector. As you explain a particular process, skill, or theory, you may move up and back, in and among your trainees (depending on the seating configuration). As trainees participate in an exercise, you will most likely move around behind them to peer over their shoulders or slide in next to them to assist with a particular task.

This flow of movement around the training room is vital to catch and maintain the trainees' interest. Every time you move to a different section of the room, you change the dynamics of the learning atmosphere. Rather than being simply a presenter, you become a facilitator. A trainer/facilitator who moves confidently, purposefully, and dramatically is much more effective than one who doesn't move at all, moves in a predictable and mind-numbing fashion, or appears hesitant and awkward.

Most wooden or misdirected body movements are caused by muscular tension. If you feel awkward and stiff, you're probably going to move awkwardly and stiffly. Like actors, trainers also can suffer from stage fright, especially when teaching a class they've never taught before or a group of trainees they've never worked with before. (It's also easy to get really tense when someone "important" sits in on your class to evaluate you!) This muscular tension not only can affect your ability to move effectively, it also can impair your ability to think straight.

Stanislavsky once demonstrated how muscular tension can inhibit an actor's ability to think. During a workshop at the Moscow Art Theatre, he asked his students, one at a time, to lift a grand piano. As one volunteer strained to lift only one corner of the heavy instrument, Stanislavsky suddenly instructed the sweating student to multiply 37 times 9 quickly. The student couldn't do it. Stanislavsky then asked the student to name all the stores along a very familiar street in the city. The student couldn't remember one. Stanislavsky asked the student to sing a well-known song. No response. To describe the taste of the student's favorite dinner. Nothing. To remember the smell of a favorite perfume. The student just grunted.

When the student finally let down the corner of the piano and rested for a moment, he was able to respond accurately to each of Stanislavsky's questions. "So you see," said Stanislavsky, "that in order to answer my questions you had to let down the weight, relax your muscles, and only then could you devote yourself to the operation of your five senses" (*An Actor Prepares*).

Trainers conducting all-day (or even week-long) seminars cannot afford to let muscle tension become overall physical rigidity. You've got to learn to relax!

## Relaxation

Stage actors typically practice a variety of backstage relaxation exercises prior to "going on." Such exercises also can help trainers to calm down, psych up, and get ready to rock and roll. Try this one yourself.

Inhale deeply, filling each part of your body, inflating it like a balloon—arms spread, chest expanded, legs open, up on your toes. Hold the air for a moment, then all at once release your breath and let your body collapse to the floor in whatever way it drops. Inhale again, inflating yourself to a standing position, then collapse again. Repeat this several times.

**Relaxation** (Group Exercise)

It's always fun to exercise with a group. Here are some warm-ups that trainers can do together.

1.  Huddle together in the middle of the playing area. On the group leader's signal, the group becomes a balloon that slowly fills with air, growing and growing until it is large and light enough to float around the room. After awhile, the balloon develops a slow leak. Slowly the balloon collapses until it is a huddled mass of players again.

2.  The entire group forms an old Model-T car. (Players can be wheels, doors, hood ornament, etc.) As the group leader turns the crank, the old car's engine slowly sputters to life and then slowly moves down the street until the engine dies again.

3.  Players form a large circle, facing out. They all turn to their right and walk around the room in a circle, leaving a space between each player. As they walk, the leader says:

    -   You are walking in the park on a beautiful spring day.
    -   You are astronauts walking on the moon.
    -   You are walking barefooted on broken glass.
    -   You are walking on hot tar.
    -   You are walking down a dark alley at midnight.
    -   You are proud show-horses in the circus parade.
    -   You are tightrope walkers in a circus.
    -   You are Indiana Jones, hacking your way through the dense underbrush of a tropical jungle. Watch out for snakes!
    -   You are a group of robots, walking to your job positions. Suddenly the robots go out of control!

4.  Partner with someone in the group. (You need an even number of participants for this exercise.) When the group leaders calls out, "people to people" face your partner. When the leader calls out a specific body part (e.g., "knees to knees"), partners immediately touch those body parts to each other. After a few of such commands (e.g., "back to back," "nose to nose,"), the leader calls out, "people to people" and each participant scrambles to get a new partner.

Nearly every book ever published on acting stresses the need for actors to learn how to control their bodies and discover what movements work most comfortably for them. Likewise, acting schools and theater arts departments require students to study a wide variety of disciplines involving body movement: dance, fencing, mime, gymnastics, yoga, t'ai chi, judo, karate, etc.

The same advice holds true for trainers. If you want to feel more comfortable about your stage presence in the classroom, take dance classes and work out regularly. Dance will teach you coordination; a good workout will keep you in good physical shape. You don't have to be Mikhal Barishnikov or Jane Fonda to be an effective trainer; you just have to feel comfortable with your own body.

# Adding Appropriate Gestures and Expressions

Once their bodies are warmed up and free of muscular tension, stage actors typically participate in exercises designed to help them explore a wide variety of gestures and facial expressions. To overcome wooden arms and deadpan faces, actors practice the art of pantomime.

The term *pantomime* has had several different (although related) meanings throughout theatrical history. The *Oxford Companion to the Theatre* lists seven definitions, ranging from Classical Greek actors who played all the parts in a production ("pan" means "all" in Greek; "mimos" is the origin of our word "mimic"), to traditional British Christmas entertainments (described as "pantomime-style" acting) with stock characters (the "pantomime horse," for example) and recognizable actions. Ask a British actor to improvise a pantomime, and you'll get something akin to what Americans would identify as "vaudeville"—broad gestures and loud, artificial-sounding dialogue (with lots of audience participation routines). Ask an American actor to pantomime a scene, and you'll get something akin to a Marcel Marceau performance—no voice, just mimed gestures.

In this book, we'll use this definition of pantomime from the *New American Heritage Dictionary:* "communication by means of gesture and facial expression."

Actors and trainers aim for the same goal: gestures and expressions that add to, rather than detract from, the presentation. "Suit the action to the word, the word to the action," said Hamlet to the Players. Easy for Hamlet to say since he wasn't standing in front of a skeptical group of first-level line managers about to endure an eight-hour seminar entitled, A Total Quality Approach to Valuing Diversity and Managing Change while Thriving on Chaos. How is the trainer to know which gestures are suitable, which facial expressions appropriate?

You can't choreograph effective gestures—unless your goal is to come across as a Las Vegas lounge act. Interestingly, the ancient Thespians thought differently, and invented the school of *chiromania*, Greek for the study of gestures (from "chiro" meaning "hand"). In many cultures, such ritualized theatrical traditions still exist (such as Chinese Opera, Japanese Noh Theatre, and Native American dances). But in modern theater, no one expects every actor who plays Stanley Kowalski in "A Streetcar Named Desire" to use exactly the same gestures as Marlon Brando used in the 1948 Broadway production. Likewise, the trainer teaching the managers will be expected to appear natural and spontaneous—and not remind the audience of an animated figure in a Disneyland display.

Appropriate gestures should punctuate your words; they should not send a message all their own. Trainers who do not move at all, who stand frozen in the "front fig leaf position" for hours on end, send this message: "It's all right to close your eyes and sleep, because there's certainly nothing interesting to look at here. Maybe you'll learn by osmosis."

At the other extreme, trainers who move too much—who pace erratically or flutter their hands through the air—send a different but equally disturbing message to the audience: "You won't be able to look here for long without feeling nauseous."

No gestures, no facial animation makes for a boring trainer. Too many gestures, too animated a face makes for a distracted audience. The goal is to reach middle-ground.

The following exercises will help you explore a range of effective gestures and facial expressions.

If you really want to see yourself as others see you, videotape yourself periodically and evaluate how you move in front of a class. To concentrate solely on body movement, gestures, and facial expressions, watch the tapes with the sound turned off. Then hit the fast-forward scan button, and watch yourself move at high speed. Any gestures that you make repeatedly will be obvious immediately, and you'll discover "tics" you may not have been aware of before. Work on eliminating these tics for a month or two, and then videotape yourself again to check your progress.

Ron Hoff, author of *I Can See You Naked*, has developed another useful way for you to determine your natural versus artificial gestures. "Stand in front of a full-length mirror [or video camera] with a large book in each hand," Hoff says. "Then talk. At times, you'll raise one hand or the other in a gesture even though the books are heavy. Those are the real gestures. Save them. Eliminate all others. Those are nervous gestures."

**War and Peace**

Divide participants into two groups. Each group lines up on opposite sides of the playing area facing each other. They are all statues in a magic museum. On one side of the room there are statues of war— ugly, mean, ferocious statues. On the other side of the room there are statues of peace—serene, contented, happy statues. Once all the participants have assumed their positions, the group leader says, "This is a magic museum. At the stroke of midnight, all the statues will come alive and begin moving slowly toward each other. When they meet in the center of the room, the statues of war will slowly turn into statues of peace, and visa versa. Ready? It's now midnight, and the statues will come alive!" This game can be continued with more opposites (e.g., light versus heavy, plenty versus famine, etc.).

**Pass the Object**

Participants sit in a circle, and one of them is handed an imaginary object (e.g., a baby bird, a lit match, etc.). That person holds the object, examines it, suggests its shape and texture through his or her gestures and facial expressions, then passes the object to the person on his or her right. Each repeats the action until the object has been passed all around the circle.

**Pantomime in Pairs**

Participants divide into pairs. Each pair then picks a piece of paper from a hat (or takes one from the group leader) on which is written the name of an everyday object (e.g., a blanket, cooking utensil, etc.). Partners then take a few minutes to work out a short pantomime that involves using the object. Both partners must use the object in some way. The rest of the class tries to guess what the object is.

**Snap**

Participants divide into pairs. Everyone practices the following five faces:
1. open-mouthed smile
2. close-mouthed smile
3. frown
4. tongue sticking out
5. ghoul face.

The players then sit or stand back to back. On the count of three, each player quickly turns around and makes one of the five faces. If the partners' faces match, the partners cry, "Snap!" The objective is to match three faces in a row.

**The What Game**

Participants sit in a semi-circle. One player comes forward and begins a simple activity (e.g., raking leaves, painting a house, baking a cake, etc.). When the other players think they know what the activity is, they do not guess out loud. Rather, they come forward and assist the first player in the activity in any way they wish. (They also can become inanimate objects.) The activity continues until all players have joined in. —Adapted from Viola Spolin's *Improvisation for the Theater*.

**Speakers and Hands**

Participants choose partners and decide who will be the "speaker" and who will be the speaker's "hands." The person designated as "the hands" stands behind the speaking partner, extends his or her arms through the speaker's, and provides all the hand gestures as the speaker speaks. (The speakers clasp their hands behind their backs.) Players then go "on stage" in groups of four, one "speaker and hands" meeting another "speaker and hands" to act out a simple improvisation. Suggestions for improvisations include the following:

- A student confronting a teacher about a poor grade.
- A traveler buying an airline ticket.
- Two children on their way to the dentist.
- The mothers of the bride and groom at the wedding.
- A bank-robber and a bank-teller.

# Keeping Your Focus

Actors and standup comics must develop their powers of concentration for two primary reasons: to create and sustain a believable persona and to deal effectively with any unplanned surprises.

Trainers need to concentrate during the training session in order to build and maintain a strong rapport with their trainees. Like the standup comic or the public speaker, your focus and energy must be directed outward toward the audience, not inward toward the pit of your stomach. Only when you focus all your attention on listening and responding to your participants will you know when and how to adjust your training objectives to meet their needs.

For the actor and the standup, concentration is also the secret to timing. How long should you "hold for a laugh" after the punch line? It depends on the audience. (You have to really listen to them.) How long should you take to build to the punch line? It depends on the audience. (You have to really watch them closely and read their body language accurately.)

Standups also concentrate to maintain control. The best way to deal with a heckler is to concentrate all your energy on the rest of the audience. Are they on the heckler's side? (Then you may have to go with the heckler's flow for a bit.) Are they on your side? (You can let the heckler have it back in kind—or better.)

Trainers rarely encounter actual hecklers, but they frequently have to deal with "difficult" trainees. (More on this in Act Three.) By concentrating on those trainees who are not being difficult, you can usually devise an effective way to defuse the situation. The secret is never to let the difficult trainee blow your concentration.

But what if some other crisis occurs? Anyone who has acted on stage, no matter how limited their theatrical experience, usually has several horror stories to relate about the time a fellow actor missed an entrance, or the phone rang at the wrong time, or the set fell over, and on and on. Such stories may be hilarious in the retelling, but they surely weren't so funny when the actor suddenly had to deal with the problem in front of an audience.

In the theater, actors are taught never to "break character." If you are playing Hamlet, for example, and one of the flats (fake walls) holding up the castle of

Elsinore suddenly falls on top of you in the middle of your "To be or not to be..." soliloquy, you are not supposed to cry, "Oh, no! What am I going to do now?" Nor are you supposed to turn to the audience and profusely apologize for the collapse. Heavens, no. You must stay in character! You must continue your soliloquy, using the force of your brilliant characterization and amazing powers of concentration to drag the audience's attention away from the set (Perhaps something was indeed "rotten in the state of Denmark"?) and back to Hamlet's existential dilemma.

Trainers have similar horror stories. Overhead projectors frequently break down; flip charts collapse; students enter class late or leave early; beepers go off at the most inconvenient moments; pages in the training manuals mysteriously disappear; and so on. Without focus, the training session flounders. Without concentration, the trainer is unable to skip nimbly over intermittent distractions and keep the session on time and on track.

Concentration helps the actor (or trainer) avoid the "slings and arrows of outrageous fortune." To illustrate this precept, Stanislavsky liked to tell his students a Hindu tale about a Maharajah who devised a rather unusual test to determine who would be his next minister. The Maharajah announced that the successful candidate would be the man who could walk around on top of the city walls, holding a dish filled to the brim with milk, without spilling a drop. A number of would-be ministers attempted the feat, but were quickly distracted by the shouts and gestures of the spectators (not to mention the presence of the firing squad), and they spilled the milk every time.

> Then came another, whom no scream, no threat, and no form of distraction could cause to take his eyes from the rim of the bowl.
>
> 'Fire!' said the commander of the troops.
>
> They fired, but with no result.
>
> 'There is a real minister,' said the Maharajah.
>
> 'Didn't you hear the cries?' the new minister was asked.
>
> 'No.'
>
> 'Didn't you see the attempts to frighten you?'
>
> 'No.'
>
> 'Didn't you hear the shots?'

'No. I was watching the milk.'

In order to "watch the milk" (meet the session's training objectives) successfully, trainers must learn to channel their focus. The following exercises provide a variety of opportunities for enhancing your concentration skills.

Here are two exercises that Stanislavsky used to help his acting students improve their powers of concentration:

1.  All stand. Move your right arm forward, then up, then to the side, and then down. Do the same thing with both arms, but move the left one movement after the right. Then repeat the exercise while walking in a circle.

2.  Participants count together to 30. They all clap their hands once when a number includes or can be divided by three. Then they repeat the exercise but clap when a number includes or can be divided by five. If the number can be divided by both three and five, they clap their hands three times.

In his book, *Creating a Character*, Moni Yakim describes a very intense concentration exercise called "Follow the Left":

The group forms a circle. The leader stands in the center and chooses a group member to initiate a vocal sound and repeat it over and over. The player immediately to the right of the initiator picks up the sound and joins in unison. The next player to the right then joins in, and so on around the circle.

The leader then chooses a second initiator—the player to the right of the original initiator. Everyone continues as before, making the new sound around the circle. After a round or two, the leader designates a new initiator, but this time without waiting for the sound to complete the circle. Then the leader picks another initiator, then another, then another, more quickly each time.

The players must concentrate on always repeating the sound of the person to their left, no matter how quickly the leader chooses a new initiator nor how noisy the group becomes.

(Variations: The group leader starts a physical gesture, rather than a vocal sound; the leader starts a gesture and a sound.)

We sometimes lose focus because we rely too heavily on all our senses. Take one of those senses away (e.g., sight), and you'll find that your power of concentration becomes mightily focused. This revised edition of the children's game, "Blindman's Bluff," provides an great opportunity to explore the powers of your other senses:

The participants divide into two groups and sit in two lines at opposite sides of the playing area. Two players (A and B) are blindfolded. An object (e.g., a shoe) is then placed somewhere in the playing field. Player A's objective is to find the object, while player B's objective is to find player A. The game ends when either player A finds the object or player B finds A.

(Note: To prevent the blindfolded players from hearing where the object is placed, the other players should make noises at the same time.)

## Concentration Exercises

(Group Exercise)

In the theater, actors participate in group sensitivity exercises to enhance their abilities to focus on their fellow performers. The same exercises can help a group of trainers develop the ability to concentrate on the energy level of their trainees—in other words, to be tuned in to their audience's mood.

1.  All the players huddle together in the corner of the room. They must be quiet so they can listen to each other's breathing and feel each other's presence. When they are all ready (no other signal is given), they separate and walk normally to the other side of the room.

2.  Participants stand in two lines, back to back and shoulder to shoulder. They must concentrate on sensing the others around them. When they are all ready (again, there is no other signal), they are to lift their right arms above their heads and bring them back down.

3.  The players huddle together at one end of the playing area, facing a real or imaginary door through which the Queen of England is about to enter. When they are all ready (no external signal is given), they take a deep breath and shout, "Long live the queen!"

Here are two children's games that can really help trainers practice their powers of concentration, develop keen observation abilities, and increase their sensitivity toward others.

**Who Started the Motion?**

One participant is "it" and must leave the room or cover his or her eyes for a few moments. The rest of the players stand in a circle, and one of them is chosen to be the leader. The leader then begins a simple movement (e.g., snapping fingers, nodding head, etc.). All the players proceed to imitate the leader, who can change the movement whenever he or she feels like it. The person who is "it" returns and stands in the middle of the circle in order to try to guess who the leader is. When "it" guesses correctly, the leader becomes the new "it" and is sent from the room while a new leader is chosen and the game continues.

**Matthew, Mark, Luke, and John**

Players stand in a circle and number off Matthew, Mark, Luke, John, One, Two, Three, Four, etc. Then they learn this rhythmic sequence: "Hit your right leg with your right hand, hit your left leg with your left hand, snap the fingers of your right hand, snap the fingers of your left hand" (a four-beat count). The object of the game is a form of verbal tag. On the snap of the fingers (the two-count), one player in the circle must say his or her name or number and the name and number of another player in the group. Before the next rhythmic sequence is completed, the second player must repeat his or her name or number and the name or number of a third player. Any player who fails to pass to someone else in the sequence or who loses the beat, loses his or her place and moves to the lowest place (next to Matthew). All players in between move up one place and assume a new number or name.

## Scene 5

# Making It All Work: Improvising

When stage actors want to practice all the techniques they've learned—how to project and add variety to their voices, how to relax their bodies, how to add appropriate gestures and facial expressions, and how to concentrate and focus on the energy of the group—they are ready to explore the art of improvisation.

When you improvise, you have to think on your feet in response to changing circumstances and unforeseen events. The very word, "improvise," comes from the Latin *improviso*: "im" = not; "providere" = foreseen. When you can't stick to the script, you must improvise.

Actors learn to improvise for two reasons: to explore their range of physical actions and vocal skills before they appear on stage, and to learn how to deal with shifting circumstances as they occur during the course of a production.

Trainers also must be able to improvise since they must adjust their performance to meet the changing needs and expectations of their trainees. Like standup comics, they must be aware of audience feedback constantly. Do most of the participants seem to be nodding off? Time for improvisation! Add an activity or announce an unplanned break. Are the trainees confused? Improvise! Make your point another way. Think of a hypothetical example or devise an on-the-spot role-playing exercise. Running out of time? Jettison a particular activity or cut an exercise. Session too short? Add an activity.

To improvise, you must be flexible and able to adjust instantly to unforeseen circumstances. If you can't be flexible, you will always be in danger of losing your train of thought, your cool, and eventually your trainees.

I have included the following exercises so that you can practice all the skills presented in this section: body movement, concentration, pantomime, and vocalization. The objective of these exercises is to help you discover how creative you can be when you're "on."

## Improvisation

(Individual Exercise)

Imagine you are conducting a training session. Make a list of all the things that you can possibly think of that could go wrong. Then imagine what you might do under such circumstances. If you can devise something humorous to do, all the better!

# Situations for Improvising With Groups

When groups perform an improvisation, they need situations to act out. Such professional "improv" groups as the "Who's Line Is It, Anyway?" performers typically ask the audience members to come up with situations for them to improvise. Here are some sample situations an audience might devise:

- Passengers are on an airplane; someone notices that one of the engines is on fire.

- Passengers are on a train; one passenger is carrying a briefcase that is ticking.

- Irate patients have been waiting a long time in a doctor's office.

- Mountain climbers have been stranded in a blizzard.

- Impatient business executives are stuck in an elevator.

- People are going through airport security; one bag contains a shrunken head.

- A robber holds up a bank.

- Silly teenagers make noise in a library.

- A group of drunk conventioneers is told that the hotel is full.

- The trainees attempt to take over the training session.

If you're working with a group of trainers, ask them to devise their own improv situations, particularly ones that would be relevant to a training session. For example, an improv situation for trainers might go something like this: A group of trainees has just been taken hostage by a disgruntled company vice-president who has just been laid off.

To improvise, all you need is a "generating circumstance" to get the group going. The rest is up to them.

Here are some improvisation games that performers on "Whose Line Is It, Anyway?" play:

### Changing Emotions

Participants pair off, and each pair is given a situation to improvise. The leader then asks the audience for a list of different emotions. Each time the leader rings a buzzer, the players must change to the next emotion while continuing to improvise the same situation.

### Party Quirks

One participant is chosen to be the host or hostess of a party in his or her home. The other players each have been given a card on which a certain "quirk" has been written (e.g., "thinks he's a duck," "a jealous lover," "an alien being," etc.). One by one the players with the quirks enter the party and greet the host. The host must try to identify which quirk a particular party guest is exhibiting.

### Standing, Sitting, Bending

Three players are given an improvisation. As they carry out the scene, one player must always be sitting, one must always be standing, and one must always be bending over. As soon as one player shifts position, the other two must compensate immediately.

Viola Spolin, pioneer American proponent of theater games as a means to self-discovery and the author of *Improvisation for the Theater*, created the "Who Am I?" game:

Player A is seated on stage. Player B enters. B has a pre-planned, definite character relationship with A (see list below), but has not told A what it is. By the way B relates to A, A must discover who he or she is and then react appropriately until the scene is finished.

Sample relationships:

- teacher/student
- husband/wife
- babysitter/child
- vacuum cleaner salesperson/homeowner
- police officer/criminal
- news reporter/U.S. President
- doctor/patient
- fortune teller/customer
- fan/movie star
- lion tamer/lion

If the trainers in a group feel at all uncomfortable with improvisation, then try the game of Gorilla Theater. (It's practically impossible to feel embarrassed when participating in this game since the objective is to act silly! And people who have difficulties moving their own bodies in front of an audience usually have no problem moving like some sort of animal.)

Participants divide into groups, and each group is given a suggestion for an improvisation. All the group members act out the scene, speaking English, but moving and gesturing like gorillas.

Variations: Frog Theater, Fly Theater, Fish Theater, Elephant Theater, etc.

# Act Three: It's Show Time!

# Objective

The really exciting thing about a "live" performance is that you can never be 100 percent sure of anything once you "take the stage." This uncertainty, of course, is the major cause of stage fright, but it's also the primary source of energy—that rush of adrenalin that tells you that you're "on."

In this section you'll practice some techniques for dealing with training situations as they occur. You'll review some of the ways standup comics establish rapport with their audiences, and you'll learn how to use "callbacks" to enhance humor and reinforce learning. You'll also explore some strategies for dealing with "difficult" trainees (the training world's version of hecklers).

For both trainers and standup comics the key words are flexibility and control. You must be flexible enough to adjust quickly to any shift in your training plans, from calling for a break earlier than you had scheduled to adding another exercise for a group that just doesn't seem to be getting the material. Simultaneously, you must always stay in control of the proceedings, from keeping the session on time and on track to dealing with any "hidden agendas" of any participants.

"There ain't nothin' like live theater," a play-going Texas cowboy once told me after a community theater production in which the actors had overcome a myriad of technical goof-ups to deliver a stirring, emotionally satisfying performance. It's the immediacy of the moment, the thought that you are participating in an event that is happening right now, before your very eyes with no tape delay, no editing, and no retakes. We're all in this together.

This is your moment. Read on.

# Interacting With Your Audience

It takes two to interact: a performer and a spectator. Indeed, the very word "inter-act" implies a give-and-take situation, an equal sharing of energy, and a mutual participation in the moment.

Even in the theater, where actors typically perform behind an invisible "fourth wall" that separates them from their audience, this sense of mutual participation is more important to the success of the production than any other theatrical element. Jerzy Grotowski, founder and director of the Polish Laboratory Theatre, argues in his book, *Towards a Poor Theatre*, that the actors and the audience are the only necessary elements of a theatrical performance. All others are superfluous. Costume and sets, music, lighting effects, the text—all can be dispensed with. "So we are left with the actor and the spectator. We can thus define the theater as *what takes place between spectator and actor*."

Viola Spolin agrees: "The audience is the most revered member of the theater. Without an audience there is no theater. Every technique learned by the actor [or trainer], every curtain and flat on the stage, every careful analysis by the director, every coordinated scene, is for the enjoyment of the audience. They are our guests, our evaluators, and the last spoke in the wheel which can then begin to roll. They make the performance meaningful."

For standup comics, this inter-action with the audience is critical to the success of their act. Standups "work" their audiences. They ask them questions, they challenge them to respond, they deal with hecklers, and—most importantly— they listen and wait for the audience's laughter, the feedback that tells them that they've touched a nerve or hit a funny bone. Every comic knows that the audience can make or break a performance. On a good night, the audience may howl with laughter or burst into spontaneous applause. On a bad night, the audience may titter politely or self-consciously clear their throats. What "works" for one audience on a particular night may "bomb" with a different audience the next day.

Nowhere is audience interaction more critical than in a training session. We trainers emphasize this interaction by the very terminology we use. We don't call the people who attend our training session spectators; we call them *participants*.

Like comics, trainers depend on audience interaction to determine if the training is working. And because they are different people, with different needs

---

and interests, trainees always keep the trainer guessing. The material presented at one site on a particular day with a specific group of trainees may come across like gang-busters. People may be enervated and involved. They may learn skills they can apply back at work, and they may give the trainer all "5s" on the course evaluations. Two weeks later at a different site on a different day with a different group of trainees, the session may drag, participants may nod off or simply leave, and the evaluations may indicate that the training "did not meet participants' needs." Same trainer, same material—but different people, a different time and place, and different results.

Such certain uncertainty can drive you mad, unless you consciously think of your trainees as participants, rather than as passive spectators. Like the standup comic, you must treat them not as enemies but as co-conspirators in a scheme to learn something. Like the stage actor, you must consider your audience to be "fellow actors" who, as John Gielgud notes in his biography, *Early Stages,* help the actor on stage "improve a performance, keep it flexible and fresh, and develop new subtleties as the days go by." The actor (and, by extension, the trainer) "learns to listen to them, to watch them (without appearing to do so), to respond to them, to guide them in certain passages and be guided by them in others—a never-ending task of secret vigilance."

Because stage actors typically act behind an invisible "fourth wall" separating them from their audience, they rarely get a chance to mingle before or during their performance. (At the most, they can peep through the stage curtains to see "who's out there." This is considered highly unprofessional behavior, and I myself have never done such a thing, of course. Ahem.)

Trainers and standup comics, on the other hand, can mingle like mad. In fact, pre-session mingling is a very useful practice for trainers. They can welcome participants into the "performance space" (the training room) as they arrive, offer some refreshments, and establish an atmosphere of relaxation, trust, and enjoyment—all elements conducive to learning.

This "trainer as host" role also is useful for identifying potential problem participants. (See "Dealing With Difficult Trainees," page 108.) If people have been "sent" to the class or if they obviously are upset about something, a few minutes of chit-chat just may be what you both need to get to know each other and reassess any negative first impressions. You might actually win a convert before the class begins. Or you might merely realize that a real jerk has signed up for the training and that you'll have to deal with this person for the next six or seven hours. But at least you won't be surprised later on when you ask for volunteers for an exercise and the "trainee from hell" sighs loudly and refuses to participate.

Before class begins, if you sense that the majority of the trainees do not want to be there, you might want to try direct confrontation, as consultant Ken Blanchard once did:

> I was talking to a group once, I was getting no energy back from them. So I stopped the talk and said, "Let me give you a little feedback; who cut off your nerve endings? I feel like I'm doing all the work. Something is going on here. Is there anybody willing to share what is going on here?"
>
> They told me they were forced to go to these seminars every year and nothing ever happened to them, they were just a waste of time as far as they were concerned, they would rather be back at work. So I told them to go back to work. "There is no point in being here if you can't focus in." A few went back. But the rest who stayed were ready to learn, or at least shocked into giving me a chance. (Quoted in Lilly Walters' book, *Secrets of Successful Speakers*.)

An extreme case, perhaps, but certainly a good example of interaction!

# Establishing Immediate Rapport

When you establish a rapport with someone, you build a "relationship, especially one of mutual trust or emotional affinity" (*New American Heritage Dictionary*). You "get in on the same wavelength" with them and become partners in achieving a mutual objective.

Standup comics know the importance of establishing immediate rapport with their audiences. As Sam Cox, developer and director of The Comedy Gym Workshop, says, "It is essential to establish a strong rapport with the audience within the first two minutes you are on stage. This is done by opening up and being natural with the audience. You must connect directly with people in the audience. You must relate honestly and genuinely with them. They won't buy your act if you're full of crap."

So how do standup comics do it? They acknowledge the audience, thank them for being there, and ask them questions. Then they use the audience's responses as springboards to their prepared material. For example, as Cox points out, a comic might ask an audience member what he or she does for a living. If the audience member replies that he's a doctor, the comic might then say, "Oh, you're a doctor? You know, I went to see my doctor last week. He gave me six months to live. I told him I couldn't pay the bill. So he gave me six more months."

Trainers use precisely the same technique when asking participants in a training session to introduce themselves, tell where they work and what they do, and then describe what concerns they have about the session's topic, or what particular skills they hope to learn from the training session. In this respect, trainers have a definite advantage, time-wise, over standup comics. The comic must establish rapport within minutes, since the performance is usually so short. In an eight-hour workshop, trainers can afford to take as much time as they need to get to know their audience.

## Ask Questions

To establish rapport, you can ask your audience specific questions: "So, Jerry, you're a manager at XYZ Corporation. What exactly do you do?" You can ask the audience rhetorical questions: "Can I assume that you're all concerned about how the reorganization plan will affect you personally?" You can ask hypothetical questions: "Suppose you had to make a formal presentation to upper management, and, at the last moment, you discovered that there was a mistake on one of your prepared transparencies. What would you do?" When you ask questions, you get immediate feedback. When you ask questions, you establish immediate rapport.

# Asking Questions To Establish Immediate Rapport

(Individual/Group Exercise)

Resist the urge to begin your next training session with a long-winded disquisition on your background and credentials, or on the course's training objectives. Don't start from where you are; start from where they are. In the space below, list any specific, rhetorical, or hypothetical questions you could ask to begin any training session you may conduct:

# Maintain Eye Contact

Trainers have another definite advantage over standup comics. They can actually see their audience!

Standups usually perform with a spotlight in their eyes. They can barely make out the people in the front row; the people in the back of the room are just vague, shadowy shapes. When you're performing standup comedy, you can direct your questions only to the few audience members you can actually see. You relate to the rest of the audience solely by the sound of their response (laughter, hopefully).

Trainers can usually see everybody in the room. You can tell at a glance whether Joan in the back row is asleep, or whether Mike on the right side has a question or complaint. Eye contact is a very powerful tool for establishing rapport. Don't overlook it. (Pun intended.)  Don't ask a specific question and then break eye contact with the person answering the question. Not only is this rude, but if you break eye contact, you also will miss a great opportunity to assess your respondent's state of mind. When you look at your participants, you can "read" their true feelings.

The best way to ascertain that you are making effective eye contact with your audience is to videotape yourself in an actual training situation. Review the tape and watch your own eyes. Do you tend to focus exclusively on one side of the room? Do you appear to be talking over the heads of your audience? Do you look like you're delivering a memorized speech, or do you look like you're really talking to the people in the room? The eyes are the windows of the soul, as the saying goes. Without eye contact, rapport is impossible.

# Using the Callback Technique

What makes us laugh? The unexpected and strange. What makes us laugh even harder? The expected and familiar. We love to see it coming a mile away. If it was funny the first time, we'll probably think it hilarious the second time. This delight in recognition is the basis of the callback technique.

Here's an example of a callback used by Mike Robbins, a Comedy Gym comic: He starts by telling the audience that his mother and father weren't the best of parents. When as a kid he ran away from home, his parents had his picture posted on the back of cans of Spam. Later in his act, he says that his parents never hired a baby-sitter for him—they just wet his lips and stuck him on the living room picture window. Neighbors thought his family had a big aquarium. Even later in his act, Robbins says he used to wave at girls as they passed by his house. "Who's that in the aquarium?" one girl would say to the other. "Oh, that's the Spam kid."

Comics can include callbacks in their prepared material, but whether or not they actually will use a prepared callback in performance depends totally on the audience's response. You see, the rule for a callback is this: The bit must get a laugh the first time. If it doesn't, you certainly don't want to call it back again for another moment of silence!

What works even better for the comic is to call back information gathered during the opening rapport-establishing part of the routine. Spontaneous callbacks are most effective for maintaining a connection with the audience and for making them howl with laughter.

Trainers have numerous opportunities to use callbacks during a training session. If you begin your session with an information-gathering exercise, you'll have lots of bits to refer to later in the class. For example, recently I was conducting my one-day grammar class for participants at a large manufacturing company. The company was undergoing a huge expansion project, and the class was taking place in temporary trailers, seemingly miles from the participants' actual work areas. Parking was a mess. No one knew where to park, and everyone was afraid of parking illegally and getting towed. (I found all this out during the first 15 minutes of class.)

This irritating (but not necessarily insurmountable) situation became a "running joke" throughout the day. When I needed to demonstrate on the white board what a simple sentence was, I wrote, "I parked my car in the green lot." To demonstrate a compound sentence, I wrote, "I parked my car in the green lot, and I got a ticket." A complex sentence? "I parked my car in the green lot, but since I have a blue permit, I got a ticket." Later in the day, I wanted to illustrate the active voice ("I parked my car in the wrong lot.") and the passive voice ("My car was towed."). I could have used any examples to illustrate my points, but my participants giggled gleefully at the parking references that I had called back. (By the way, the humor also defused much of the irritation that everyone had been feeling when they started the class in the morning.)

## Callbacks

(Individual/Group Exercise)

Think back to a recent training session you conducted and list below any bits of information you gleaned from your participants that you could have used as callbacks later in the session.

# Dealing With Difficult Trainees

Standup comics call them hecklers. These are the audience members who have decided to participate without being asked. They make inappropriate comments, interrupt the comic, and try to steal away the spotlight. Not courageous enough to go up on stage themselves, they prefer to shoot off their mouths in the darkness, hoping to see the comic sweat. They are the bane of the comic's act, and they are legion.

Hecklers are such a common occurrence on the comedy club circuit that comics are cautioned to prepare for them, to have a ready arsenal of stock comebacks to fire off whenever a heckler rears his or her ugly head.

Here are some stock anti-heckler retorts used by standup comics: If the heckler interrupts you with a mild crack, cup your hand around the microphone and say, "Security, table twelve. We have a live one." If someone shouts at you incoherently from the back of the room, try "Sir, would you slur that a little louder," or "Just feel free to shout out meaningless crap anytime you feel like it, ma'am." If the heckler is particularly insistent, appeal to the rest of the audience: "Ladies and gentlemen, we live in the greatest nation in the world, and what makes it so great is that it is a democracy. That means we all get to vote. So I want each of you to vote right now. By your applause, how many of you think this woman should JUST SHUT UP!"

These are great, huh? If you're a standup comic, you can use these as often as you like. You can enjoy the thrill of squashing a heckler like a bug, and of asserting once and for all your power over the audience.

If you're a trainer, you can't use any of these. Sorry. Your job is to educate people, to involve them in the learning process. If you put them down, you'll alienate them. They won't learn anything. Plus, you'll probably alienate the rest of the audience as well. Then no one will learn anything.

Besides, you will rarely meet a pure heckler in a training situation. What you're most likely to experience is that creature known as the "difficult" trainee: the participant who challenges your expertise, who answers your questions with a sarcastic or irrelevant remark, or who distracts or disturbs the other trainees.

There are several things you can do to deal with a difficult trainee, none of which involve putting the person down in any mean-spirited or nasty way.

# Use Your Standup Skills

The Scenario: You're up in front of a class, training away. Gradually you become aware that two trainees in the back of the room are not paying any attention to your "extremely important" remarks. In fact, they're whispering to each other, perhaps giggling, perhaps passing notes back and forth. They are your "Difficult Trainees" (DTs). How do you get them to behave without making enemies of them?

1. **Make eye contact.** While you continue to speak to the group as a whole, look directly at one, then at the other, until you catch their eyes. Hold the eye contact until they break it off.

   For most polite people, this is usually all you need to do. Remember that the other trainees in the class will tend to look at what the trainer is looking at, particularly if the trainer holds the eye contact for a significant length of time—longer than a few seconds. When the DTs look up and see that everyone in the room is looking at them, they'll probably stop fooling around immediately.

2. **Move towards them.** Alas, some people can't take a hint. If the DTs continue to be distracting, try moving towards them. Literally walk over to them—still talking to the group as a whole—and deliver your remarks from in front of the DTs, or right behind or right next to them. Once again, with all the other eyes in the room looking their way, most DTs will cease and desist as long as you're physically close to them. (This is an old elementary school teacher technique for keeping order in the classroom. It works just as well in the business world.)

3. **Involve them.** If even physical proximity doesn't work, then you're going to have to get the DTs involved in the training itself. If you've done your homework, if you've analyzed your audience before the training session, you should know some background information about each of your trainees already.

   So, for example, if your DTs are Bob and Carla, and you know that Carla is a long-time company employee with experience in, say, soldering techniques, and you're conducting a certification class in electrostatic discharge, you might lure Carla away from her conversation with Bob by saying, "Carla, I know you've had some experience with the concept of 'latent damage' in the work you've been doing here, right?" (If you are right, Carla will start paying attention immediately. After all, you're now talking about her.)

Or you can include Bob in a hypothetical example: "OK, to illustrate this, let's suppose a technician in our company—someone like Bob, for example—was having a problem with soldering a wire to a particular terminal and . . . ."

Make either Bob or Carla part of the example you're using to make your training point and you will most likely regain—and keep—their attention.

4. **Defuse the situation with humor.** Kind humor. Sweet humor. Silly humor. Nothing mean or vindictive. In your best "Miss Thistlebottom" voice you say, "Well, well, well. It seems that Bob and Carla have some information that is more important than the subject of our training session today. Bob and Carla, would you like to share your information with the rest of the class? Mmmmmmm?"

If you're funny enough, if you can act the part well enough, your trainees—Bob and Carla included—will laugh (and get your point). But caution: This option only works if you really know your trainees well, and if you've already established a rapport with the group. Otherwise, this option will backfire. Bob and Carla will be angry, the rest of the class will be embarrassed—for them and you—and you'll lose any chance you ever had of teaching them anything.

## Dealing With Difficult Trainees    (Individual/Group Exercise)

Everyone who has ever trained, taught, or performed before a live audience has horror stories to tell about disruptive, disturbing, or just downright obnoxious audience members. In the space below, describe one of your own training horror stories, and describe what you did to deal with the situation (or what you should have done.) If you're working with a group, share the stories and suggestions for alternative ideas.

# Epilogue

# Epilogue

Every actor and standup comic knows that the success of a performance depends in great measure on the response of the audience. Thus, actors talk frequently about "how the house was tonight." Were they responsive? Where they "intelligent"? Or (shudder) were they "dead"? It's easy for actors to blame a lackluster performance on their audience.

Trainers also are prone to emphasize their participants' lack of participation, rather than the trainer's own lack of energy. It's always somewhat painful to admit that the fault may indeed lie with the performer, rather than the performance. Trainers, standup comics, and actors wear their hearts on their sleeves when they perform. Their egos are on the line. Criticize an actor's or trainer's "act," and you criticize the person as well.

Thus actors, standups, and trainers share the same ambivalent response to criticism. We all want to know how we did, and what the audience thought of us; however, we don't want to hear that the audience found us boring, or inappropriately dressed, or hard to understand. We say we want the dark truth, but we'd rather have the little white lies.

# Dealing with Criticism

Bad reviews can have a devastating effect on both an actor's and a trainer's career: An actor who is slammed in print may wind up "box office poison," unable to get another role for many years. A trainer who receives mostly negative evaluations from a group of participants may lose future contracts or classes. No wonder we examine those end-of-course evaluations with fear and trepidation.

But we must not take all reviews too seriously. To paraphrase St. Francis's prayer, we must recognize the performance behaviors we can change, accept the behaviors we can't change, and have the wisdom to know the difference between the two. It's really a matter of degree. If only one person in the class complains on the evaluation that you were "too theatrical," just ignore it. If half the class, however, complains that you were too animated, or moved too much, or were distracting in any way, then you have some work to do to improve your stage presence. (Run, do not walk, to the nearest video camera and get yourself taped.)

For a trainer, the worst thing a participant can say about your performance is that you were boring. ("The instructor spoke in a monotone." "The instructor never moved from behind the podium." "The instructor was too stiff, too formal, too static, too dull.") It is true that sometimes participants fall asleep in a training seminar because the room is too hot, or they ate too heavy a lunch, or they didn't sleep last night, or they're sick, etc. If one person is having difficulty staying awake, it may not be any fault of yours. Ignore it. But if most of the participants are demonstrating severe MEGO (My Eyes Glaze Over), then it's probably your fault and you need to use the acting techniques described in this book to wake them up and get them learning again.

The standup trainer keeps the audience awake. The standup trainer is not boring. The standup trainer makes participants wonder how the time went by so fast. The standup trainer can make any topic interesting, no matter how dry or technical.

# Resources for Further Standup Training

Anyone who really wishes to can learn to be a standup trainer. You may not be able to learn "the divine fire of genius," as the great American actor E.H. Sothern (1859-1933) described the actor's art, but you can "sharpen and polish the weapons wielded by talent. . . . Harsh, throaty, or nasal voices can be made musical; vile pronunciation can be made perfect; awkward bodies and limbs can be made graceful; restlessness can be trained to repose; even taste and tact and observation of color, form, and sound can be quickened and cultivated."

If you want to hone your standup skills, as well as your theatrical abilities, enroll in a standup comedy workshop (contact the Comedy Gym at 1-800-700-JOKE), or take the stage yourself during a local comedy club's "open mike" night. The experience will teach you much about developing comic material, and will give you a new appreciation of how much easier it is to be funny when you don't actually have to be funny!

For stage experience, check out your local community theater. Audition for the next play, especially if it is a comedy. Once you've experienced the paralyzing stage fright that comes from having to memorize your lines, you'll never again be scared in front of a group of trainees who just expect you to talk to them like real people.

You also can learn by watching and imitating other trainers, using Laurence Olivier's method for continual improvement: "I watch all my colleagues for different qualities that I admire, and I imitate them and copy them unashamedly." (ASTD international, technical & skills training, and chapter conferences provide perfect opportunities for learning from your colleagues.)

Whatever you do, continue to videotape yourself periodically, using the following checklist to evaluate your own performance.

## Performance Evaluation Checklist    (Individual/Group Exercise)

Answer the following questions after watching yourself on tape, conducting an actual—not mock—training session with real participants. If you're working with a group, use this checklist to evaluate each other's performance and provide helpful feedback.

❑ Evaluate the trainer's voice. Did the trainer project well enough so that everyone could hear? Was there enough vocal variety to be interesting? Does the trainer have any vocal problems that need further improvement?

❑ Evaluate the trainer's body movement, gestures, and facial animation. Were there any movements that were distracting to the audience? Does the trainer have any "tics" that need to be eliminated?

❑ Evaluate the trainer's concentration and improvisation abilities. Did the trainer ever lose focus during the session? Why? Was the trainer able to think fast and respond quickly to any changes or interruptions?

❑ Did the trainer establish immediate rapport with the audience? How? Note any "callbacks" the trainer may have used, and evaluate their effectiveness.

❑ Did the trainer deal effectively with any difficult trainees? In what ways?

❑ Did the trainees seem to enjoy the class?

❑ Did the trainees learn what they were supposed to learn?

# Curtain

At the end of David Mamet's play, *A Life in the Theatre*, an actor named Robert stands alone on the stage and addresses an imaginary audience, raising his hand to stop the imaginary applause.

> You've been so kind. . . Thank you, you've really been so kind.
> You know, and I speak, I am sure, not for myself alone, but on
> behalf of all of us. . . all of us here, when I say that these . . .
> these moments make it all . . . they make it all worthwhile.

Robert knows that the struggle to entertain will always be worth it, as long as we receive direct positive feedback from those we wish to please.

If, at the end of your next training session, you know that you kept them awake, you kept them interested, and you taught them something, then you, too, will deserve a standing ovation (even an imaginary one).

Take a bow.

# Additional Reading

*Actors on Acting*. Ed. Toby Cole & Helen Krich Chinoy. New York: Crown, 1970.

Adler, Mortimer J. *How To Speak, How To Listen*. New York: Macmillan, 1983.

Adler, Stella. *The Technique of Acting*. New York: Bantam Books, 1988.

Artaud, Antonin. *The Theatre and Its Double*. New York: Grove Press, 1958.

Barker, Clive. *Theatre Games*. London: Eyre Metheun, 1977.

Barrault, Jean-Louis. "Rules of Acting" in *The Theatre of Jean-Louis Barrault*. Translated by Joseph Chiari. New York: Hill and Wang, 1962.

Berry, Cicely. *Voice and the Actor*. New York: Macmillan, 1973.

Brockett, Oscar. *History of the Theatre*. Boston: Allyn & Bacon, 1968.

Brook, Peter. *The Empty Space*. New York: Avon Books, 1968.

Delsarte, Francois. *Delsarte System of Acting*. Translated by Abby L. Alger. New York: Edgar S. Werner, 1893.

Devine, Betsy and Cohen, Joel E. *Absolute Zero Gravity: A Collection of Jokes, Anecdotes, Limericks, and Riddles Revealing the Funny Side of Physics, Biology, Mathematics, and Other Branches of Science*. New York: Simon and Schuster, 1992.

Eble, Kenneth. *The Craft of Teaching: A Guide to Mastering the Professor's Art*. San Francisco: Jossy-Bass, 1976.

Friedman, Paul J. and Yarborough, Elaine A. *Training Strategies from Start to Finish*. Englewood Cliffs, NJ: Prentice-Hall, 1985.

Gielgud, John. *Early Stages*. New York: Macmillan, 1939.

Growtoski, Jerzy. *Towards a Poor Theatre*. New York: Simon and Schuster, 1968.

Hagen, Uta. *A Challenge for the Actor*. New York: Charles Scribner's Sons, 1991.

Hoff, Ron. *I Can See You Naked: A Fearless Guide to Making Great Presentations*. Kansas City, MO: Andrews and McNeel, 1988.

Lambert, Clark. *Secrets of a Successful Trainer.* New York: John Wiley & Sons, 1986.

Matheis, Marianne. "Getting a Foot in the Door," *Training and Development Journal.* April, 1989.

Moore, Sonia. *The Stanislavsky System.* New York: Viking Press, 1965.

Munson, Lawrence C. *How To Conduct Training Seminars.* New York: McGraw-Hill, 1984.

Piscator, Edwin. "Objective Acting," in *Actors on Acting.* Ed. Toby Cole & Helen Krich Chinoy. New York: Crown, 1970.

Rigg, Diana, compiler. *No Turn Unstoned: The Worst Ever Theatrical Reviews.* New York: Doubleday, 1982.

Scher, Anna and Verrall, Charles. *100+ Ideas for Drama.* Oxford: Heinemann Educational Books, Ltd., 1975.

Spaid, Ora A. *The Consummate Trainer.* Englewood Cliffs, NJ: Prentice-Hall, 1986.

Spolin, Viola. *Improvisation for the Theatre.* Evanton, IL: Northwestern University Press, 1963.

Stanislavsky, Konstantin. *An Actor's Handbook.* Edited and Translated by Elizabetha Reynolds Hapgood. New York: Theatre Arts Books, 1963.

Stanislavsky, Konstantin. *My Life in Art.* Translated by J.J. Robbins. New York: Theatre Arts Books, 1948.

Stanislavsky, Konstantin. *An Actor Prepares.* Edited and Translated by Elizabeth Reynolds Hapgood. New York: Theatre Arts Books, 1936.

Yakim, Moni. *Creating a Character: A Physical Approach to Acting.* New York: Backstage Books, 1990.

# About the Publishers

## The American Society for Training and Development

Founded in 1944, ASTD is the world's premiere professional association in the field of workplace learning and performance. ASTD's membership includes more than 58,000 people in organizations from every level of the field of workplace performance in more than 100 countries. Its leadership and members work in more than 15,000 multinational corporations, small and medium-sized businesses, government agencies, colleges, and universities.

ASTD is the leading resource on workplace learning and performance issues, providing information, research, analysis, and practical information derived from its own research, the knowledge and experience of its members, its conferences and publications, and the coalitions and partnerships it has built through research and policy work.

Among the many benefits of ASTD membership are

- subscriptions to *Training & Development* and *Technical & Skills Training* magazines, and *Human Resource Development Quarterly*

- special-interest Forum memberships and the quarterly *Performance in Practice* newsletter

- *The National Report, Who's Who in Training and Development,* and *Buyer's Guide and Consultant Directory*

- discounted rates to two annual international conferences and expositions

- discounted rates for select books and tapes

- discounted subscriber rates to ASTD Online, which allows you unrestricted access to electronic mail and bulletin boards, Trainlit database, *Buyer's Guide & Consultant Directory,* full-text articles, job postings, and Internet access.

For more information on available products and services or to join ASTD, please call 703/683-8100 or fax 703/683-1523.

# Creative Training Techniques Companies

Assisting trainers in achieving exceptional learner satisfaction and bottom-line results using innovative methods, concepts, and technologies is the focus of Bob Pike's Creative Training Techniques Companies.

Building trainer competencies is the goal of Creative Training Techniques International, Inc., the world's largest provider of public and in-house professional development for trainers. Over 150 seminars covering over 40 cities are held each year, modeling the best of instructor-led, participant-centered training. Many of the over 60,000 alumni of this powerful program gather for a re-fresher each autumn at a conference held in Minneapolis, Minnesota.

Bob Pike's popular train-the-trainer offerings include:

- Creative Training Techniques: 37 Ways to Deliver Training with Greater Impact and Effectiveness

- Training for Impact: Needs Assessment, Training Transfer, & Evaluation Methods for Bottom-Line Success

- Creating High Impact Visuals and Interactive Learning Activities: Practical and Proven Graphics & Games for Dynamic Trainers

- High Impact Soft Skills Training: How to Increase Performance and Create Positive Change!

- Techniques & Tricks for Trainers: 119 Magical Attention Management & Review Tools to Make Your Sessions More Powerful

For a catalog of public seminars, or information on in-house sessions, call (800) 383-9210 (USA) or (612) 829-1954.

# Creative Training Techniques Press

A convenient source of creative games, graphics, music, "how-to" books and videos, and presentation tools that enhance trainer effectiveness are available by phone or mail order through Bob Pike's Creative Training Techniques Press.

Three trainer development videos by Bob Pike are "High Impact Presentations," award winning "Creative Training and Presentation Techniques" and "Creative Training Techniques Newsletter in Action."

For a product catalog, call (800) 383-9210 (USA) or (612) 829-1954.